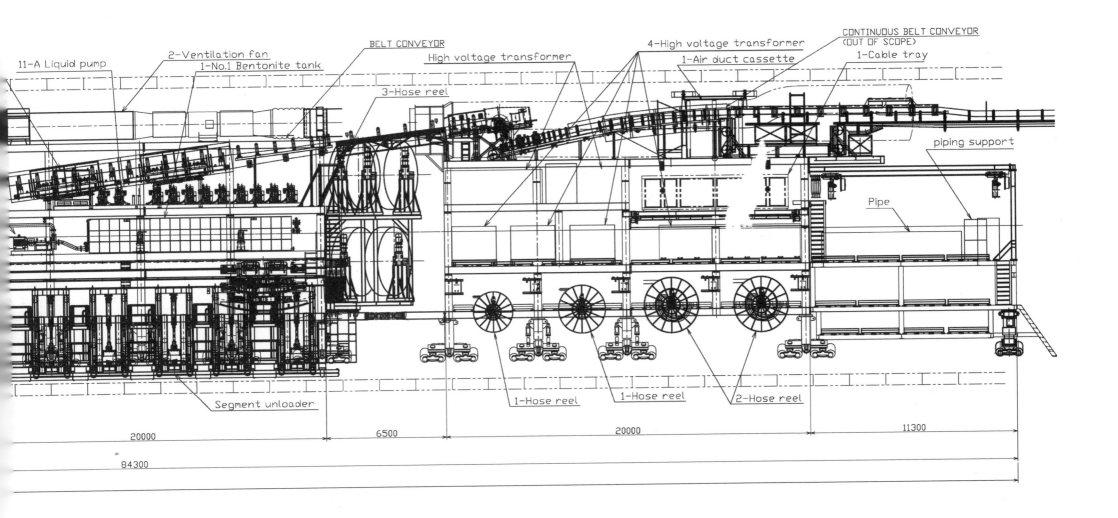

Building Seattle's State Route 99 Tunnel

SUPERTUNNEL

Journey from light to light

Building Seattle's State Route 99
SUPERTUNNEL
Journey from light to light

Copyright ©2020 by Catherine Bassetti

All rights reserved, worldwide. No part of this book may be reproduced in any form or by any electronic or mechanical means, including information storage and retrieval systems, without permission in writing from the author.

ISBN: 978-1-7343359-0-3

Cataloging in Publication:
Library of Congress Control Number: 2020903772

Photography, Design, and Production: Catherine Bassetti
Introduction and major contributor: Gregory Hauser, Deputy Project Manager, Seattle Tunnel Partners

Commentary: Reiner Decher, Lorne McConachie, and David Sowers (WSDOT)
Additional statements: Scott Nicholson (CalPortland); Jeff Horst (Foss Maritime); Shinji Ogaki (Hitachi Zosen Corporation); Brian Russell (HNTB); James Lindsay (Master Builders); Peter Steinbrueck (Port of Seattle); Chris Dixon (Tutor Perini); Mike Mingura (Tutor Perini); Nathan Burch (Tutor Perini); and Labor Union representatives: Marge Newgent, Derek Patches, Michelle Helmholz, Rick Hicks, Ryan Hyke, Marilyn Kennedy

Selected text and commentary contributed by project crew members: Jeff Huber, Will Campbell, Cody Heck, Jamie Willard, Ismael Martínez, Justyn Workman, Jerry Roberge, Enoch Lish, Perla García, Lisa Miller, Chris Lucas Roscoe, Shawn Overby, Marisa Roddick, Marcel Oedraogo

Back cover photo: Takayuki Iwamuro, Electrician (Hitachi Zosen Corporation)
Interior cover drawings: Courtesy of Hitachi Zosen Corporation
Second printing / photo enhancements

Entry quotation: from the book entitled <u>To Engineer is Human</u>, by Henry Petroski

Disclaimer of Liability: This book is a photographic documentation of a Public Works Transportation Project, the construction of the SR 99 Tunnel, Seattle, Washington, USA. Images of all property and persons depicted in this book are for the sole purpose of documentation and not subject to liability for claims of any kind relative to their use.

To engineer is human
- Henry Petroski

Building Seattle's State Route 99 Tunnel

SUPERTUNNEL

Journey from light to light

CATHERINE BASSETTI

CONTENTS

INTRODUCTION	8
COMMENTARY	12
SEATTLE: PORTAL TO THE PACIFIC	14
STATE ROUTE 99 AND THE ALASKAN WAY VIADUCT	16
PLANNING AND DESIGN	22
BERTHA	25
MANUFACTURING BERTHA	26
UNDERGROUND JOURNEY BEGINS	30
BERTHA HALTS UNDERGROUND	38
ACCESS SHAFT	40
SPOTLIGHT: ACCESS SHAFT FOREMAN	52
BERTHA BREAK-IN	56
BERTHA RESCUE	64
BERTHA REPAIR AND RETURN	70
SPOTLIGHT: TOPLANDER	81
BUILDING THE HIGHWAY WHILE DRIVING THE TUNNEL	84
CONCRETE	90
INTERIOR TUNNEL WALL	92
SPOTLIGHT: TEAMWORK	96
SPOTLIGHT: ERECTOR OPERATORS	100
MINING RESUMES	104
SPOTLIGHT: COMPRESSED AIR WORKER	108
SPOTLIGHT: TUNNEL BORING MACHINE PILOT	110
CUT AND COVER ZONES	112
TUNNEL ALIGNMENT	116
TUNNEL MONITORING	118
SOIL TREATMENT AND PROCESSING	122
SPOTLIGHT: WATER TREATMENT FACILITY	124
MOVING THE MUCK	126
LABOR UNIONS AND TRADES	134
MOVING ON UP: CARPENTER TO SURVEYOR	139
SPOTLIGHT: SENIOR SITE ADMINISTRATOR	140
RIGHT HAND MAN: SKILLED LABORER	141
A FAMILY AFFAIR: CARPENTER TO FOREMAN	142
AMAZING JOURNEY: LABORER TO SAFETY MANAGER	143
SITE OPERATIONS BUILDINGS	144
BERTHA ARRIVAL AND EXIT	152
BERTHA DISASSEMBLY	162
SPOTLIGHT: MECHANICAL WELDER	166
TUNNEL SAFETY	172
TUNNEL INAUGURATION	180

JOURNEY

INTRODUCTION

The Alaskan Way Viaduct (AWV) was a two-deck elevated concrete roadway that carried State Route 99 along the waterfront of Seattle. Built in the early 1950's it was already approaching the end of its life. In 2001 the Nisqually earthquake damaged the AWV. The road was repaired and strengthened and reopened with restrictions, but it was apparent that a replacement highway was needed. Years after the earthquake, the State of Washington, the City of Seattle, and King County all agreed the best option would be a bored tunnel large enough to move both directions of SR 99 traffic beneath Seattle. This double-deck tunnel would run from the stadiums in the south part of the city, north to the Seattle Center area near the Space Needle.

The Washington State Department of Transportation (WSDOT) requested proposals from qualified contractors. In October 2010 two Joint Venture (JV) contractors submitted proposals to WSDOT. Seattle Tunnel Partners, JV (STP) composed of Dragados USA from Spain and Tutor Perini Corporation from California, USA were selected. In December 2010, WSDOT awarded the contract to STP to build the new tunnel and highway. The tunnel itself was to be 9,273 feet long, with the two-deck highway built inside the tunnel as the tunnel was being driven—allowing STP to deliver the tunnel and highway to WSDOT a year earlier than the other proposal. The contract amount of the proposal was $1.4 billion with a completion date of December 2015, allowing STP to deliver the tunnel and highway to WSDOT nearly a year ahead of WSDOT's required completion date.

STP selected a Tunnel Boring Machine (TBM) to be manufactured by Hitachi Zosen Corporation of Osaka, Japan. The TBM was designed to be 57.5 feet in diameter and erect precast concrete segments with an inside diameter of 52 feet for the tunnel lining. The concrete segments were two-feet thick, weighing over 37,000 pounds each. It took ten segments to complete one ring, which covered 6.5 feet of tunnel.

On October 12, 2011, STP issued a purchase order to Hitachi Zosen for an Earth Pressure Balance Tunnel Boring Machine, or EPB TBM, to be delivered in April 2013.

In January 2012, Dragados USA contacted me about going to work for the STP JV as the Deputy Project Manager in charge of building the tunnel for the new highway. I accepted the position and started working for STP on March 30, 2012. This was the beginning of a challenging and stressful assignment which was ultimately a very successful and gratifying project.

The TBM that Hitachi Zosen manufactured was handed over at a ceremony in Japan in December 2012 and named "Bertha" after Bertha Knight Landes, the first female mayor of Seattle. The TBM was delivered to the project site in April 2013 and assembled in the launch shaft south of King Street. On July 30, 2013, Bertha began her journey north and the replacement for the Viaduct began. During the time that the TBM was mining, SR 99 remained in service except for the two weeks when the TBM mined under the AWV, when WSDOT decided it was best to shut the AWV down, because nobody knew exactly what might happen as Bertha tunneled below the footings for the Viaduct. As it turned out, the tunneling had virtually no impact or detrimental effect to the existing AWV, or any building or utility along the 9,273 lineal feet of tunnel that was mined by Bertha below Seattle.

After the launch in July 2013, the tunnel crews were getting familiar with Bertha, how she reacted to steering, and the different soils she was tunneling through. There were issues to attend to, but this is normal for new TBMs (and all tunneling projects). During the night shift on December 5th, 2013 the TBM began to slow and the night shift operators quit early. On December 6th, the day shift attempted to advance the machine by increasing thrust and torque. The limits for temperature in the bearing were being exceeded and the TBM shut itself down to prevent further harm to the systems. Unknown to us at the time, but eventually realized, Bertha had suffered major damage to her main bearing and the seals that protect the bearing from intrusion of soils, debris, and water. The cause of the breakdown is, as of this book's publication, part of a legal dispute and cannot be speculated upon here. The necessary repairs resulted in more than two years of delay to the mining of the tunnel.

To accomplish the repairs, a 120-foot deep shaft was excavated to access the TBM and remove the cutter head and drive assembly for further investigation of the damage and potential repair options. It was eventually decided that the outer seals, main bearing, and other damaged parts of the TBM would be repaired or replaced. The main bearing was replaced, and the cutter head was reinforced to ensure that such a condition would not occur again. While the TBM was down for these needed repairs, additional modifications and enhancements were made to the TBM, as is common in the tunneling industry, to reduce the chance of further delays that would impact the completion of the Project after the restart of mining. By the end of 2015, the TBM had been repaired. The access shaft was backfilled and the TBM mined ahead to the north face of the shaft.

As agreed with WSDOT, STP worked 24/7 until the TBM was safely past the Viaduct, which WSDOT closed to traffic as a safety precaution. By May 12, STP had mined the 67 rings (= 435.5 lineal feet of tunnel) to get past the Viaduct, all without any impact to the Viaduct. It was then reopened to traffic and the crews went home for a well-deserved long weekend.

On May 16, 2016, the crews returned and worked diligently to complete the tunnel drive to the North Operations Building at 6th Avenue and Thomas Street in Seattle.

The TBM holed into the shaft at 6th and Thomas on April 4, 2017, exactly on line and grade, in grand condition. Sadly, Bertha could not be removed in sections that would allow her to be rebuilt and mine again. This marvelous piece of tunnel equipment was cut apart and removed to enable completion of the SR 99 thoroughfare to allow traffic under the City of Seattle.

The highway was completed, tied into the existing roadways at the North and South connections to SR 99 and opened to traffic in February 2019. Today you can drive through this engineering marvel and witness first-hand what has been accomplished for the State, the City, and the County.

ABOUT THE AUTHOR

Catherine Bassetti, Photographer for Seattle Tunnel Partners, was responsible for documenting all aspects of the tunnel construction and supporting job sites. The TBM Bertha was a monument to engineering and an example of what can be accomplished with dedicated workers and a committed Owner who needed a replacement for a damaged and vital roadway. Catherine commemorates Bertha and the tunnel that Bertha created.

Catherine also captures the spirit and determination of the craft workers and how they added to this record-breaking project. Catherine was a regular fixture of the project from the time she joined STP, until after the TBM Bertha completed her drive and the interior road decks were installed. Because of her understanding of the efforts of everyone on the project, she photographed some of the most difficult and demanding portions of this work. Her photos are truly works of art of this engineering tour-de-force.

Through Catherine's devotion to thoroughly record the achievements and progress of the project, this book is a tribute to the men and women who worked hard to complete this vital piece of transportation for all who live in the region.

This book celebrates the TBM Bertha, the tunnel that Bertha excavated, and the highway that was built inside that tunnel. This civil engineering project has set a new measure for what can be accomplished for transportation systems and projects all across the USA and is an example of what can be done to improve our transportation infrastructure. Catherine's book is a grand documentation of all that has been accomplished.

Gregory Hauser
Deputy Project Manager
Seattle Tunnel Partners

COMMENTARY

Major changes in the Seattle cityscape do not happen often. Yes, new buildings are built; they change the skyline and exacerbate the traffic. Such changes are relatively gradual as companies new and old evolve, move in or out. Not so gradual is the change brought on by a community mandate to free the waterfront of its wall—the acoustic and visual barrier of a viaduct carrying traffic on the artery that was old US 99, now State Route 99. The Viaduct had to be demolished due to safety, but its traffic-moving role not demoted. Ancient glaciers have limited what we can build to travel between north and south and we really need old 99 to help.

A tunnel is brutally efficient without convenient exits, but the vulnerability from earthquakes eliminated the opportunity to travel with views of the harbor and mountains. The beauty will surely be recovered as the city reclaims its waterfront.

So here we are, several years after the promised project, with a tunnel that really works and takes its place among Washington State's infrastructure innovations as one of the grandest. We built big suspension and floating bridges, as well as tunnels in soft soils or gravel, without disturbing those above them. The SR 99 Tunnel under Seattle with its gigantic size is a monument for the people who built it and the leaders who managed it. The road to innovation is never easy. It challenges the abilities of people and can teach lessons not only on what to do or not do, but also how to manage such enterprises. Their names may not be in the vocabulary of people who travel the tunnel years hence, but they will be appreciated.

The pages of this book are the image memory of Seattle's 99 Tunnel as an undertaking. These pictures contrast starkly with those of yesteryear of sweaty men working on a dark tunnel face with picks, shovels, or pneumatic drills. In all, it is a beautiful and powerful witness to the story, photographed with care and skill.

Seattle is re-imagining itself.

From my fifth-floor office above Columbia and Western, I feel as if I'm witnessing the complex choreography of a monumental dance. Progress has been understandably slow and noisy, albeit steady. Watching the emerging waterfront is fascinating—a rebirth in real time. The outlook to the Sound is no longer interrupted by a screaming ribbon of concrete. Views from the ferries embrace our vibrant history—from Pioneer Square to Pike Place Market, the giant Port cranes to the Space Needle, the downtown skyscrapers to the Great Mother, Mt. Rainier. The new tunnel dives silently beneath the stage, effortlessly carrying crosstown traffic, while the city heals itself, reconnecting with its raison d'être—the deep water of Elliot Bay. New projects enter the show from stage left and right. The seawall augurs resiliency along the verdant ecotone of land and sea, tentacles of Pike Place reach down the bluff, Pioneer Square and Belltown spawn apartments, and the waterfront park and esplanade anxiously wait in the wings to make their triumphant debut.

Enjoy the show—it only happens once in a lifetime.

This book is a look backstage. The boring of the tunnel was one of the initial acts in this great dance piece. The stage crew who designed and built the tunnel brought extraordinary imagination and dedication to this monumental project. Catherine Bassetti's photography elegantly documents this opening act.

Reiner Decher
Professor Emeritus
Aeronautics & Astronautics
Adjunct Professor, Civil Engineering
University of Washington

Lorne McConachie, FAIA
Bassetti Architects

The Washington State Department of Transportation (WSDOT) was tackling some significant projects when I joined in the fall of 1999. Tasked by the State Legislature, they included a new Tacoma Narrows bridge and a new highway corridor in Spokane. When the 6.8 magnitude Nisqually earthquake shook the region in February 2001, the replacement of the Viaduct was suddenly at the top of that list.

I began working on the Alaskan Way Viaduct Replacement Program in the summer of 2008, as various solutions to replace the Viaduct were being considered. In January 2009, the Governor directed WSDOT to explore a tunnel solution as the preferred Viaduct replacement option. Having spent most of my career working on geotechnical-focused projects, I was excited by this mandate.

The decision to deliver the tunnel as a design-build contract had a team of hand-picked WSDOT staff and consultants craft a Request for Proposal (RFP). In late 2010, WSDOT selected Seattle Tunnel Partners as the best-value proposer and signed the $1.4B contract the following February.

My role on the AWV Program and tunnel projects evolved over the next ten years. I started out focused exclusively on all things related to geotechnical instrumentation and protecting buildings and utilities. Along the way I forged relationships with staff at the City, the County, the Port, and of course with the STP. Many of these professional relationships grew into long-lasting friendships, even as the project concluded and each of us moved on to other projects or retirement.

Countless times over the course of the tunnel project something would happen that would suddenly change our thinking and push us into action, often in an unknown, unplanned direction. It could be a call from an elected official or one of our public partners. Usually it involved some late-night or weekend discussions.

The WSDOT team learned to thrive in these settings. Sometimes it was as simple as a broken utility. Other times—such as when dewatering began for the repair shaft, and unexplained ground movement quickly brought us all together—we first wrestled with the technical unknowns, and then the political and community sides of things.

After assisting with troubleshooting, the stoppage of the TBM, and then working with the City utility departments to address their concerns about dewatering impacts on their facilities, I moved into another role as one of two AWV Program deputies. In this role, I oversaw all budget and finance matters, and moonlighted as the project spokesperson on all things technical, and occasionally political.

I was once asked on camera, through all the trials and tribulations, what I liked most about the experience. I said that being part of something that was an absolute technical marvel was a thrill for an engineer. On top of that, the tunnel would forever change the landscape of the City. And finally, I said, no day was ever the same.

David Sowers
Deputy Program Administrator, WSDOT

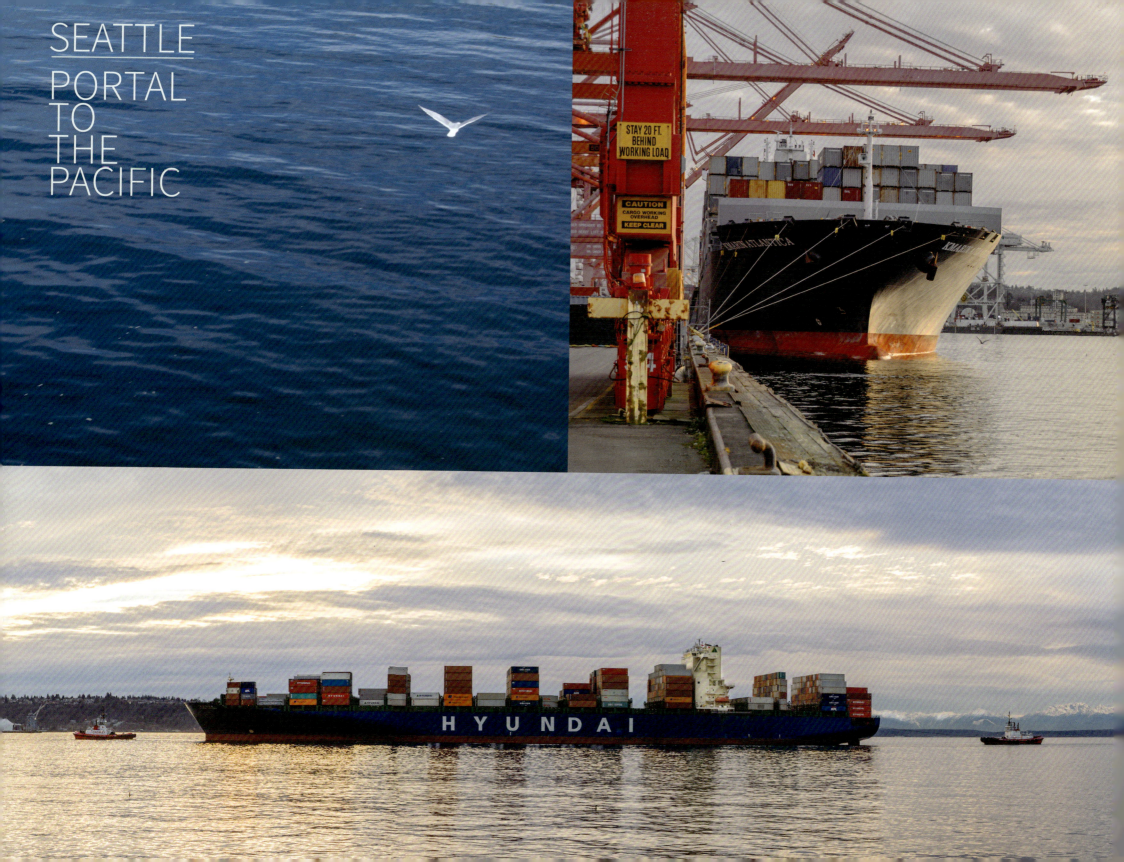

"Those who do not learn from history are doomed to repeat it." -**Santayana**

Since the buzz of Yesler's sawmill was first heard in the mid-1850's, Seattle's central waterfront has always been a bustling, noisy, chaotic place of maritime trade, warehousing, transportation linkages, and commerce. The Port of Seattle was established in 1911 by an act of the state legislature, in large part to better serve the growth of the region and bring order to the overcrowded waterfront along Railroad Avenue and the multiple competing rail lines serving the wharves. The Port of Seattle today has evolved to become the fourth largest container seaport in North America, homeport to the North Pacific Fishing Fleet and two busy cruise ship terminals with more than one million embarking passengers annually.

After the 2001 Nisqually earthquake badly damaged the near half-century old Alaskan Way Viaduct, Governor Christine Gregoire, following years of political squabbling and indecision by local officials, made the bold decision in 2009 to replace it with a two-mile, deep bore tunnel. The Port recognized it had a strategic interest in maintaining freight corridors through the highly constricted downtown and contributed $267.7 million dollars—crucial to fully funding the tunnel's $3.29 billion construction cost.

The 2001 "Rattle in Seattle" was a wake-up call, which gave us a once-in-a-lifetime opportunity to remove a monstrous urban blight and help move forward our shared vision for the city of an accessible waterfront for all.

Peter Steinbrueck, FAIA
Commissioner, Port of Seattle

STATE ROUTE 99
THE ALASKAN WAY VIADUCT

The Alaskan Way Viaduct (AWV) was originally built in the 1950s. At the time, it was state-of-the-art construction and a unique addition to the much smaller City of Seattle. The AWV carried cars and trucks going on State Route 99 from the southern industrial area to north of Seattle near the Space Needle, with off ramps to strategic locations within the City.

The AWV also provided vehicle occupants with a panoramic view of Elliott Bay, the waterfront, Puget Sound, and, on clear days, the Olympic Mountains. The AWV was a feature that drew tourists and welcomed locals who knew it offered a quick, easy ride through the City with a beautiful view.

The Viaduct was old and nearing its design lifetime when it was damaged in the 2001 Nisqually Earthquake. Initially, the AWV was closed until the State could determine if it was safe for continued traffic. Repairs and reinforcements were made to damaged sections. The Viaduct was reopened to traffic, with weight restrictions and semi-annual inspections to monitor the condition of the roadway. It was clear that a replacement was needed. Another earthquake would have been catastrophic for the Viaduct and a nightmare for traffic and commuters.

There were years of debate over what type of structure should replace the Viaduct, or if it should be replaced at all. Options from another elevated roadway, to a flyover bridge, to a tunnel were offered and discussed—it seemed endlessly. Finally, clear heads, logic, and sound engineering prevailed. The option for a single-bore, large-diameter tunnel was selected, and approved as the best solution.

This book records and details some of the efforts it took to make this solution a reality. These pages also share some of the stories of the men, women, and various organizations that participated to make this project a success. To travel through the tunnel now, along State Route 99, is an easy drive. Instead of a view of the Bay, Puget Sound, and the Mountains, riders get a look at a truly amazing tunnel built below downtown Seattle with no impact to the structures above. The result is a resilient replacement for the ailing Alaskan Way Viaduct.

Column at Pier 110 of 138, State Route 99

Riding aloft along the water's edge suddenly all was untethered and glorious and you were part of the spectacle. We'll miss this old grey highway for the lifetime of rides we've shared. Freighters and ferries glide across the Bay capped by the Olympic Mountains rising behind. There was no better introduction to Seattle than a drive along the Viaduct.

PLANNING AND DESIGN

Completion of the State Route 99 tunnel was a transformative event in Seattle's storied transportation history. It also was a breakthrough for the worldwide tunneling industry, expanding possibilities of construction size and safety. The colossal 57.5' bored diameter, nearly 2-mile-long tunnel opened to motorists on February 4, 2019.

The tunnel was one of several projects managed by the Washington State Department of Transportation to improve safety and mobility along SR 99 and Seattle's waterfront. Collectively, these projects are referred to as the Alaskan Way Viaduct Program, a $3.3 billion infrastructure program that was one of the largest in the country.

The project began with the 2001 6.8 magnitude Nisqually earthquake, which caused the double-decked elevated freeway to sink, damaging the viaduct's concrete joints and columns. WSDOT made emergency repairs to the viaduct, reinforcing the damaged columns and beams that supported the viaduct roadway. However, these repairs were only stopgaps. WSDOT knew the viaduct needed to be replaced with a new highway designed to meet current seismic standards and updated highway design criteria.

While considering how to replace the viaduct, WSDOT learned a city-owned seawall, which protects the waterfront from seismic events and tsunamis, was also failing. Timber and concrete sections were deteriorating and needed to be replaced. To create a solution that would fix both issues, WSDOT and the City of Seattle worked together to replace their aging infrastructure in a coordinated effort.

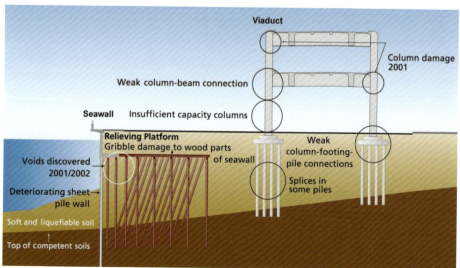

Seawall and Viaduct earthquake vulnerability. (Drawing courtesy of WSDOT)

After the Nisqually earthquake, WSDOT and local agencies studied more than 90 options for replacing the waterfront section of the viaduct. Four alternatives were assessed in the final environmental impact statement, submitted in January 2009: a bored tunnel, a cut-and-cover tunnel, an elevated structure, and a no-build alternative that would have demolished the viaduct without replacing it.

The preferred alternative, a bored tunnel, promised the least disruption to businesses and traffic during construction. It also meant a repaired and reinforced viaduct could be maintained as a vital downtown route until the tunnel opened. After the tunnel opened to traffic, the viaduct could be demolished to make way for the city's large-scale waterfront renewal effort.

In 2003, a multi-jurisdictional partnership between WSDOT, the City of Seattle, and King County was formed to deliver the project. After the National Environmental Policy Act record of decision was approved by the Federal Highway Administration (FHWA) in August 2011, the following occurred:

- The FHWA provided federal funding and ensured the viaduct replacement projects met federal regulations.
- WSDOT led the efforts to build the new SR 99 tunnel and its connecting roadways and to demolish the existing viaduct after the opening of the SR 99 tunnel to traffic.
- King County implemented transit improvements associated with the program.
- The City completed the seawall repairs concurrent with the tunneling efforts and is leading the restoration efforts for the street area.
- Infrastructure, connecting the Port of Seattle to the highway and city streets was incorporated into the project with funding from the Port.

In December 2010, WSDOT awarded a design-build contract valued at $1.1B to Seattle Tunnel Partners (STP), a joint venture of Dragados USA Inc. of New York, NY and Tutor Perini Corporation of Sylmar, California. The Bellevue, Washington office of HNTB Corporation was the lead designer and engineer of record for the tunnel. STP was responsible for the design, construction, testing, and commissioning of the bored tunnel, the north and south access structures, the tunnel systems, and all permanent structures and facilities. HNTB was responsible for the design of the tunnel liner, interior tunnel structures, the two operations and maintenance buildings, and all associated facility systems, including mechanical and electrical systems, and architectural finishes.

The north approach project was designed by WSDOT and constructed by Guy F. Atkinson Construction of Golden, Colorado. The south approaches were designed by WSDOT and the Seattle office of WSP. They were constructed by Gary Merlino Construction Company of Seattle; Skanska of New York City; Guy F. Atkinson Construction; and Interwest Construction Inc. of Burlington, Washington.

STP's winning proposal incorporated several value-added features, including a larger-sized tunnel to enhance vehicular safety and traffic operations with larger roadway clearances. With a colossal tunnel boring machine (TBM), STP's design was able to accommodate a 32'-wide roadway, which includes two 11'-wide travel lanes, a 2'-wide shoulder on the east, and an 8'-wide shoulder on the west. Vertical clearance was increased to 15' 5".

The tunnel was excavated by an earth pressure balance (EPB) TBM, which was built to control the rate at which the excavated ground was removed through the pressurized face at the front of the machine. The pressurized, or closed, face maintained ground stability and allowed operators to work in safe, controlled conditions in the tunnel.

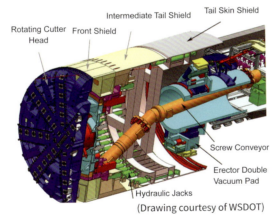
(Drawing courtesy of WSDOT)

The design and construction of the massive tunnel presented countless challenges. Two of the biggest were controlling ground deformation to protect everything above the tunnel and designing the tunnel to meet stringent safety requirements and seismic criteria. Controlling ground deformation meant controlling the volume of excavated soil, removing only the amount necessary to advance the machine, and then filling voids with grout. STP crews carefully advanced the machine as the team monitored progress and watched for any indication of settlement or movement.

HNTB designed a segmental concrete tunnel liner system in order to resist the high seismic loads and to control water leakage. The segmental liner pieces are bolted together with watertight gaskets between each segment, which were compressed during installation.

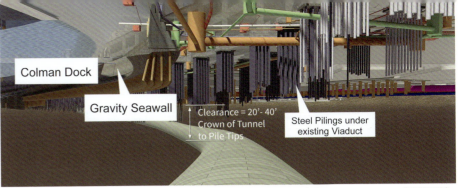
Subterranean view of tunnel alignment. (Diagram courtesy of WSDOT)

The liner design enabled the contractor to make minor adjustments and better control the tunnel's geometry—its horizontal curvature, vertical profile, and any accidental deviations caused by the TBM. A total of 10 precast segments, each 2' thick and 6.5' wide, form the one-pass lining ring and were assembled within the tail shield of the TBM. The segments that form the ring were designed so that the rotation of the ring would incrementally change the TBM's heading.

Behind the concrete-lined bored tunnel, the cavernous 52'-diameter space was simultaneously filled with the new double-decker highway. This roadway was built in assembly-line fashion, with the roadway structure assembled in sections. To connect the roadway structure to the tunnel, continuous corbels held in place by dowels drilled into the ring segments, were built. Walls and slabs were built on top of the corbels, with steel formwork that moved on rails.

Construction of the lower roadway slab was skipped to keep the lower portion of the tunnel clear, allowing passage of personnel carriers and equipment that hauled segments and materials in support of tunneling operations. The lower roadway was designed as a series of precast slabs that were post-tensioned together, so the lower road deck could be rapidly installed as part of the final steps in the roadway construction process. Because of Seattle's location in an active seismic region, the liner design met stringent operational and performance requirements. The largest expected earthquake during the design life of the tunnel has a 108-year return period. During such an event, the lining is designed to respond in an elastic manner. The tunnel materials will rebound quickly to their original shapes after the earthquake. Little, if any, damage is expected. During a rare, large earthquake, which would be on the order of a moment magnitude 9 with a 2,500-year return period, some damage of the tunnel is expected but without collapse or loss of water tightness.

Brian Russell, PE
Project Manager, HNTB

BERTHA &

THE WORLD'S LARGEST DIAMETER COMPLETED TUNNEL

Bertha, the tunnel boring machine, was the largest TBM ever built at the time it was delivered from Osaka, Japan. Measuring 57.5 feet in diameter—five stories high—Bertha was built by Hitachi Zosen Corporation.

Named after Seattle's first female mayor, Bertha Knight Landes, the machine is referred to as an 'earth-pressure balance' tunnel boring machine, or EPB TBM. This model was chosen because of the many variants in the soil and underground conditions of the tunnel drive route stretching along the waterfront and beneath Seattle's downtown district.

Bertha was specifically designed for this project and had many features unique to digging this particular tunnel. One such feature was the screw conveyor, which removed the conditioned muck from the bottom of the cutter head mixing chamber and brought it up to the conveyor belt and out of the tunnel. The screw conveyor selected by Hitachi Zosen was a ribbon-type screw that did not lift the muck as much as it allowed boulders as large as three feet in diameter to be removed from the cutter head. This was because the soil borings had indicated the presence of many such boulders. It was a specific feature designed to remove them. As it turned out, very few boulders were actually removed by the screw; most were just pushed aside by the mighty thrust force of the propel rams. Bertha had 56 thrust rams for a total thrust of 88 million pounds.

Bertha had other features that would allow her main bearing to be removed and replaced underground if needed. While she had this feature, we did not use it for the bearing replacement, as building the access shaft was much quicker and safer. Bertha was cutting-edge technology and a marvelous piece of equipment that performed exactly as intended once the repairs were made.

Gregory Hauser, Deputy Project Manager, Seattle Tunnel Partners

57.5 feet

MANUFACTURING BERTHA

HITACHI ZOSEN CORPORATION

In October 2011, Hitachi Zosen Corporation (Hitz) received an order from STP to design and manufacture a Earth Pressure Balance Shield Tunneling Machine (TBM) for the SR 99 Bored Tunnel Project, measuring 17.45 meters, the largest diameter TBM in the world at that time.

The major TBM structure was fabricated in Sakai and Ariake Works of Hitz in Japan as well as subcontracted to a factory in China. Specialty parts were procured from professional suppliers around the world such as Germany, France, Italy, Brazil, U.S.A., and China; then assembled and tested at Hitz Sakai Works in Osaka, Japan. In December 2012, 14 months from the order placement, a completion event was held and she was officially named "Bertha." She then left for the voyage to Seattle.

Excellent technology was employed. Many human and technical resources were spent to build the super big Bertha in order to achieve the client requirement to complete the tunnel mining safely and quickly under the difficult mining conditions in Seattle. For example, she is equipped with "Cutter Changing Devices" that allow the cutter bits to be changed from inside the spokes of the cutter head, making it possible to change the cutter bits safely and easily under atmospheric conditions and shorten the tunnel excavation period.

Assembly of middle body

The total weight of the TBM, including three Back-Up-Cars, is about 7,000 tons. The total length is about 100 meters (328 feet). That is too large to build inside the factory building. Thus, we built her in our dry dock by covering the dock with a large movable tent where we are usually building offshore structures. (We previously built Very Large Crude Carriers in that dock.)

After Bertha arrived at Seattle, we dispatched about 50 technical advisors to support Seattle Tunnel Partners for on site assembly. Four technical advisors were stationed in Seattle during the entire excavation period to support STP operators for mining until TBM breakthrough.

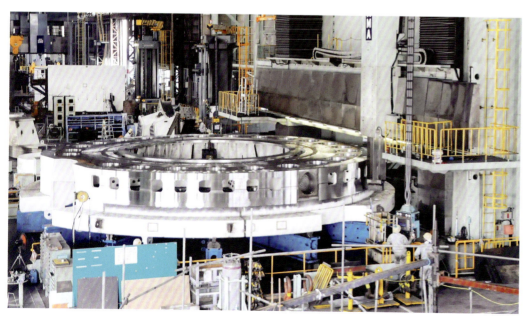

(Left) Machining of bearing block, (Above) Assembly of Cutter Driving Unit

All photos of TBM manufacturing, courtesy of Hitachi Zosen Corporation

When we faced a TBM stoppage near Terminal 48, the difficult decision was made to repair Bertha on site, in consultation with STP. The repair work was very difficult because it was necessary to remove the approximately 2,000-ton Cutter Driving Unit from the rescue shaft, then repair it on site. That was unprecedented TBM repair work anywhere in the world.

However, we undertook this difficult repair work with STP for the City of Seattle to make the SR 99 Project a success and to open the SR 99 tunnel. To do so, we gathered all of our technical capability, together with the cooperation of our subcontractors such as Mammoet, National Welding, In-Place Machinery, as well as our client STP, to overcome the difficulties we encountered during the repair work. Then we successfully completed the repair of Bertha to resume mining.

Lastly, it is our pleasure that Bertha has completed her role and the SR 99 Tunnel has opened. We are honored and proud to have been involved in this valuable project.

Shinji Ogaki
Project Manager,
Hitachi Zosen Corporation

Completion of TBM manufacture

BERTHA ARRIVAL TO PORT OF SEATTLE

On April 2, 2013, the Fairpartner, a heavy load carrier ocean vessel with Bertha on board, was greeted with full regalia entering the Port of Seattle and Elliott Bay.

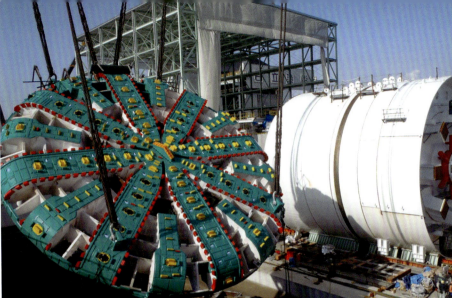
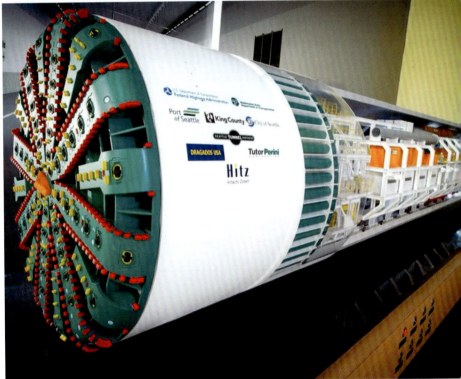

(Left) Bertha's massive cutter head measuring 57.5 feet in diameter, is hoisted to the front of the tunnel boring machine. (Lower right) A model of the full machine, including the five-story multi-level trailing gear section, was on display in Seattle throughout the project for the public to explore. (Photos courtesy of WSDOT)

UNDERGROUND JOURNEY BEGINS

Elliott Bay

South Portal Site / Tunnel Launch Zone

Pioneer Square

Stadiums

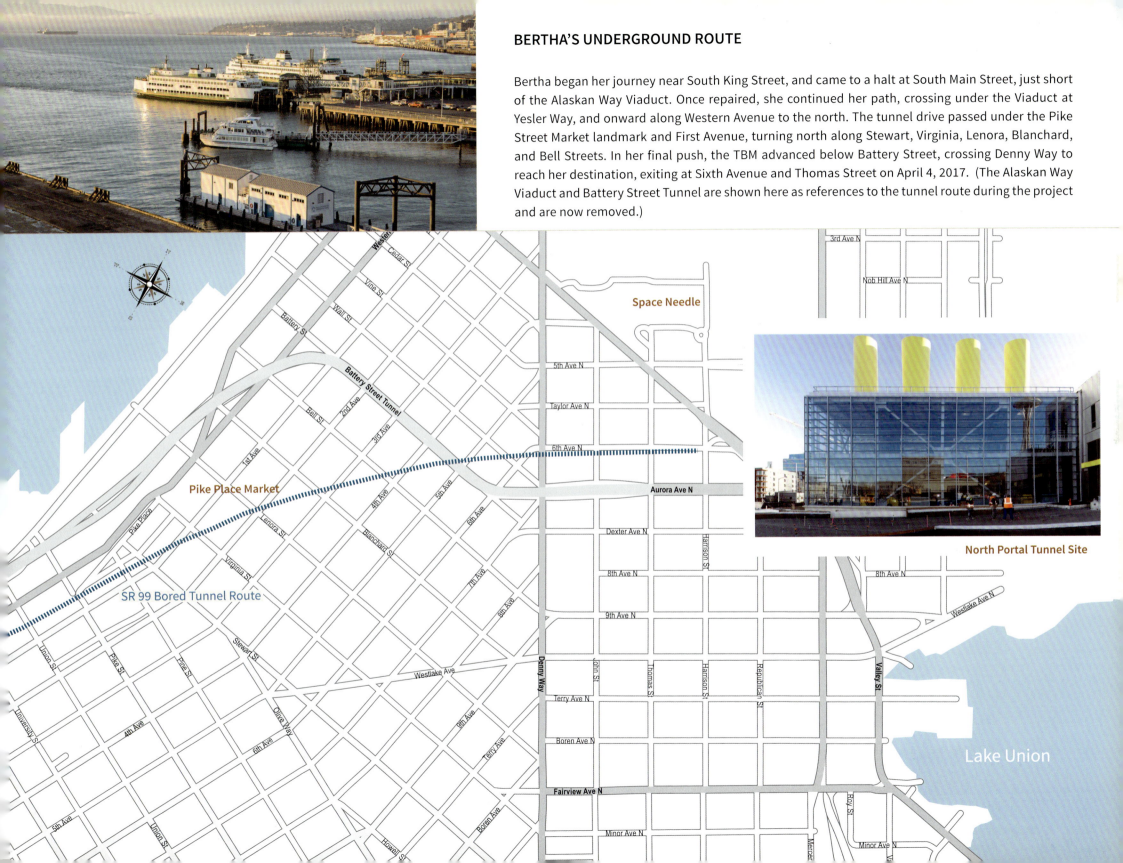

BERTHA'S UNDERGROUND ROUTE

Bertha began her journey near South King Street, and came to a halt at South Main Street, just short of the Alaskan Way Viaduct. Once repaired, she continued her path, crossing under the Viaduct at Yesler Way, and onward along Western Avenue to the north. The tunnel drive passed under the Pike Street Market landmark and First Avenue, turning north along Stewart, Virginia, Lenora, Blanchard, and Bell Streets. In her final push, the TBM advanced below Battery Street, crossing Denny Way to reach her destination, exiting at Sixth Avenue and Thomas Street on April 4, 2017. (The Alaskan Way Viaduct and Battery Street Tunnel are shown here as references to the tunnel route during the project and are now removed.)

North Portal Tunnel Site

EARLY DAYS AT TUNNEL LAUNCH LOCATION AND CUT & COVER ZONE

The tunnel 'launch zone' and adjoining 'cut and cover' area were excavated 100 feet below sea level, parallel to the piers along the southern end of Seattle's downtown waterfront. The tunnel boring machine Bertha was lowered into the shaft and began her underground journey here.

Post-launch, this area was used throughout the drive for the delivery of all materials, vehicles, and tunnel ring segments. Crews entered and exited from this end of the tunnel for the following five years.

As is protocol for most tunnel construction projects, safety precautions required that all crew and visitors be 'brassed in', by hanging their brass token on a board at the entrance to the scaffold as they entered. If an emergency should occur below or in the tunnel, the brass indicated to the safety management team which workers were underground at any given time.

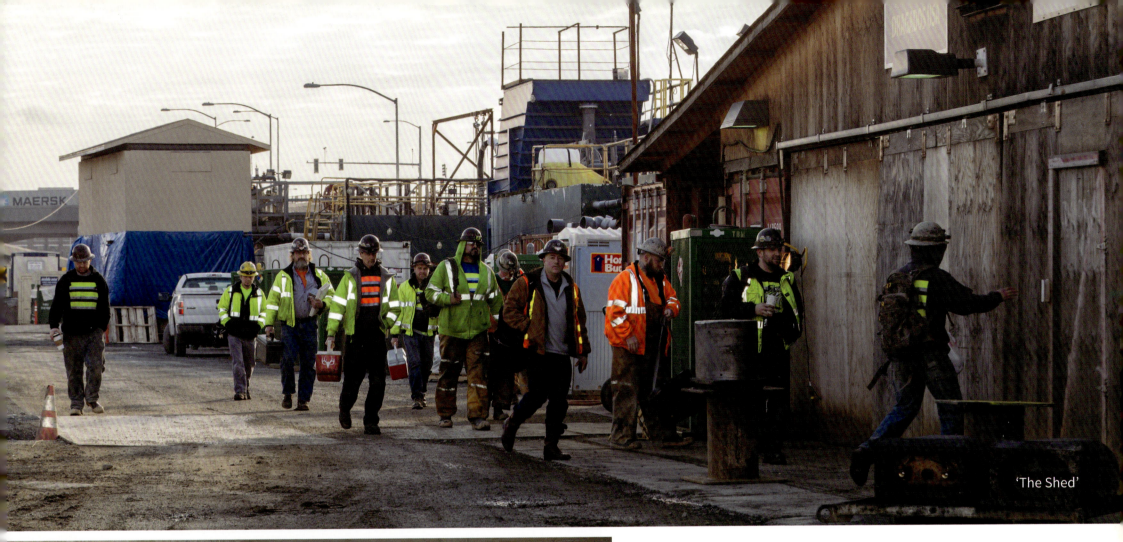

'The Shed'

(Above) A tunnel crew arrives at the work shed to discuss the day's activities. The shed, a large open space for storage of tools, parts, and worktables, was a convenient gathering place for crew members, both day and night.

(Left) View from the south end of the tunnel launch zone, leading to the 'cut & cover' partition of the project, with the mouth of the tunnel visible at the far end.

BERTHA HALTS UNDERGROUND

The biggest project risk in Washington State's new State Route 99 tunnel was at the south end, where the tunnel begins, due to extremely soft, unconsolidated soils. The challenge was to excavate through that zone without creating settlement and subsequent damage to structures and utilities. If the tunnel boring machine could mine through that initial zone problem-free, Seattle Tunnel Partners (STP) and HNTB Corporation were confident the remaining portion of the drive would be relatively risk-free.

Because of these heightened concerns, HNTB built two planned maintenance stops into the design, also known as "Safe Havens". The first stop was just beyond the TBM launch headwall, and the second was 1,500 feet into the drive, just ahead of where the tunnel would cross under the viaduct

The earth surrounding the planned maintenance stops was stiffened with cement grouting so that the contractor could bury the TBM cutter head in the fortified ground, get in front of the machine, and make any necessary repairs.

In early December 2013, the TBM had journeyed about 1,000 feet into the tunnel drive when its electric motors became overheated. An investigation revealed damage to the machine's seal system and contamination within the main bearing. Fortunately, because the machine had malfunctioned in a high-risk zone and just before the second planned maintenance stop, it was in a location where a shaft could be constructed and the TBM removed.

Brian Russell, PE, Project Manager, HNTB

(Opposite) Bertha halted here, just short of the Viaduct at Alaskan Way South and Main Street. Malcolm Drilling begins excavation for the placement of the secant pilings to encompass the Access Shaft. (Above) A crew member walks by the Pier 48 parking lot at the spot where the tunnel boring machine sits underground. (Right) Entrance to the tunnel and 'trailing gear' while Bertha was under repair.

Drawing, courtesy of WSDOT

Tunnel boring was halted for two years while STP excavated and built the Access Shaft, hoisted the machine cutter head to the surface, and disassembled it. Hitachi Zosen Sakai Works, which manufactured the TBM, repaired the main bearing and added steel supports to reinforce the interior of the machine. The TBM resumed drilling of the tunnel on December 22, 2015.

ACCESS SHAFT

The Access Shaft measured 80 feet in diameter and 120-feet deep. The shaft was designed by Brierley Associates. Malcolm Drilling installed the ten-foot diameter secant piles to support the shaft. The design and construction of this shaft was a major piece of work requiring nearly a year to excavate and build. The construction of the shaft, adjacent to the Alaskan Way Viaduct, did not interfere with the normal around-the-clock flow of traffic on the highway.

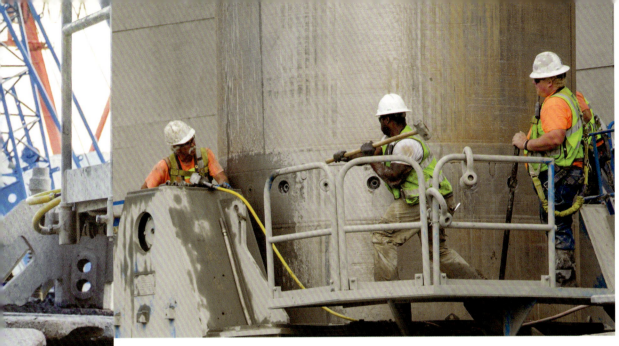

ACCESS SHAFT WALLS AND SECANT PILINGS

Secant pilings are concrete piles that overlap each other to form a continuous wall of concrete and support the opening that is dug within the ring of piles. These secant piles were ten feet in diameter and over 140-feet deep. Pilings were excavated and filled with concrete on each side of the intermediate pile. Then the gap was closed by excavating the still-green concrete and placing a pile between the previously-placed initial piles. This was very exacting work and required many pieces of equipment to install the initial piles, followed by the intermediate piles as soon as possible. Once the entire ring of secant pilings was complete, and the concrete cured, excavation of the shaft could begin.

(Left) Laborers at the base of the Access shaft at 120 feet below ground, the lowest point prior to the building of the 'cradle' platform in preparation for Bertha's entry into the shaft for repair. (Opposite) Aerial view of the Access Shaft and the traffic driving north on the top deck of the Alaskan Way Viaduct. The TBM Bertha sits hidden behind the south wall of the shaft, to the right.

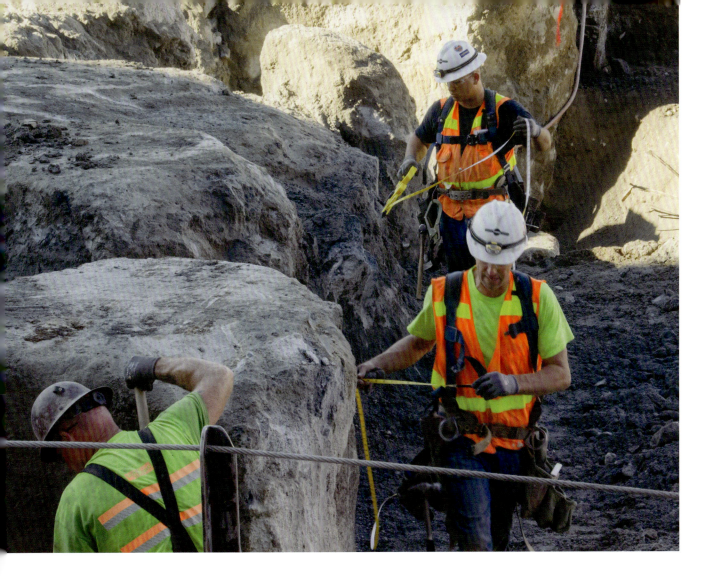

DEWATERING

Because the shaft was so close to Elliott Bay, excavation was below the water table almost from the beginning. To complete the excavation and pour the shaft invert 120-feet deep, it was necessary to dewater the ground and relieve the pressure of the water pushing upward.

A drill rig was mobilized and supported over the partially-excavated shaft. A well was then drilled about 200-feet deep to dewater the sand layer below the shaft bottom.

The well was installed, and the dewatering continued for several months until the base slab was placed, and the concrete cured sufficiently to withstand the uplift of the water.

This deep well was in addition to shallow wells installed for the initial excavation. The water from all these wells required treatment before returning to Elliott Bay.

Rescue shaft foreman, Jeffrey Huber (left), and Tunnel Superintendent, Tom McMahon (right)

SPOTLIGHT
ON THE JOB

ACCESS SHAFT FOREMAN, JEFF HUBER

Jeff on the crow's nest overlooking the 120-foot deep Access Shaft

"I was a foreman employed by the Seattle Tunnel Partners during the big Bertha project. I did everything a foreman would do in a tunnel group. There's nothing that can prepare you for a job like this. We were supposed to be in and out of there within a couple of years, but as everybody knows, it didn't happen like that. We sunk that recovery shaft in winter. It was miserable; it was cold; we were challenged every day. To watch these guys and gals perform was amazing. It was truly an honor to be their foreman. We had a great management team, we had a great crew, and I learned a lot.

The tunnel industry is thought-provoking. There were folks down there that have been doing this for longer than I've been alive. I will never forget the opportunity to have led these folks, and in earlier years, to have worked for them. It was humbling. We had a lot of challenges—we went without sleep; we slept on the job sometimes; slept in trucks or offices. We got the job done. At times we would have five-to-six contractors working on site with us, plus sub-consultants. It was a busy, busy project. If you worked down there, your life got put on hold until this machine got underway. I am very proud we did that.

No day down there was ever the same. There was no easy day; this was no 'walk in the park'. During the rebuild, the crews were running seven-days-per-week, 12-hour days. That's just what was expected. The input we received from the crew was absolutely instrumental in getting this machine back on the way. We had a lot of people with different backgrounds; everyone had a job to do; their ideas were extremely valuable. The best part of my job was arriving in the morning and seeing these crews ready to work. Then watching the night shift crew come in. All of us just came together. Everything that happened down there was because of a team effort. You come to a point in your professional life that nothing will measure up to that project, nothing."

Jeff Huber and Greg Hauser, Deputy Project Manager, Seattle Tunnel Partners

"If you worked down there, your life was put on hold until this machine got underway".

"I was involved from the very beginning, from even before off-loading the machine. It was shocking when the cutter head arrived on that ship; going up on that ship to help unload; getting everything ready. When the machine broke down, the mindset of the crew was "let's get this thing fixed and up and running". It took a little longer than what we all thought. At the end of the day, they did the job; the crew got it done.

You know, there was some controversy over the tunnel, but it doesn't matter. I had the opportunity to go to the Grand Opening, and the next day I ran the 8K marathon. I realized while running through that tunnel, "we won… we battled this out". The credit goes to the crews. Great guys and gals, great trades folks. My door is always open to them."

The crew arrives at the site to discuss the day's workflow. (Below left) Foreman, Jeff Huber, and crew with Bertha during the backfill process.

"I get asked what the best part of my job was there. I would have to say going in the morning and seeing these crews ready to work, watching the night shift crew come in, watching them just go out and make it happen."

Jeff Huber served in the Marine Corps prior to working on tunnels. He now runs his own business in the construction and environmental sector.

  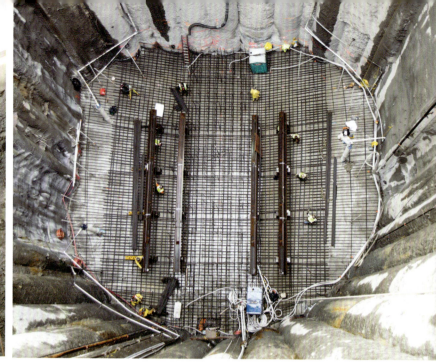

INTERIOR FLOOR CRADLE FOR BERTHA

The base slab (above right) was a massive section of reinforced concrete that would accept the weight of the TBM and support it in a stable cradle while it was disassembled and repaired. This was a major pour. The reinforcing was detailed and critical to the success of the shaft and getting the TBM repaired.

Simultaneously: crews completed the excavation, repaired secant piles that were not structurally sound, maintained the dewatering wells, formed and poured the pile cap and the shaft invert—all in a very tight site, with the Alaskan Way Viaduct in full operation immediately adjacent to the site. With each day presenting different issues, good coordination and cooperation were essential on this complicated Access Shaft site.

Everyone worked together toward the end goal—a shaft to reach Bertha and the cutter head.

Night watchman, Access Shaft

BERTHA BREAK-IN

BIRD'S-EYE VIEW FROM THE CROW'S NEST

February 19, 2015 was a long-awaited day. All hands were on deck: crews, management, engineers and personnel milled around the wide grounds at the excavation site between the Viaduct and Elliott Bay. The atmosphere was electric with anticipation.

440 days of complex planning, bold decisions, and innovative solutions had transpired since Bertha halted underground, hidden from view. This was her second debut; perhaps more dramatic than the first.

From the crow's nest, you could hear the tunnel boring machine churning behind the concrete pilings marked with bull's-eye sensors. As it grew nearer, the sound of the machine was a combination of grinding and screeching, like a prehistoric beast of the imagination, amplified by the chamber of the 120-foot shaft. Then it was silent, as the last few interior tunnel walls were placed in position. Finally, Bertha inched forward, wounded, toward her destination.

Shortly before 11 AM, a leak of steamy smoke slid through the cracks in the pilings and bits of concrete plunked into the cradle below. Then, precisely on the hour, the wall busted open from the top down, the giant columns breaking, tumbling, crashing forward, water spitting from the machine, visible for enough time to marvel at its magnificence before being covered in a billow of white dust. Over the course of the day, amidst much jubilation, Bertha turned slowly behind the bath of groundwater in the bottom of the shaft, and by nightfall her full shiny silhouette was visible once more for the world to see.

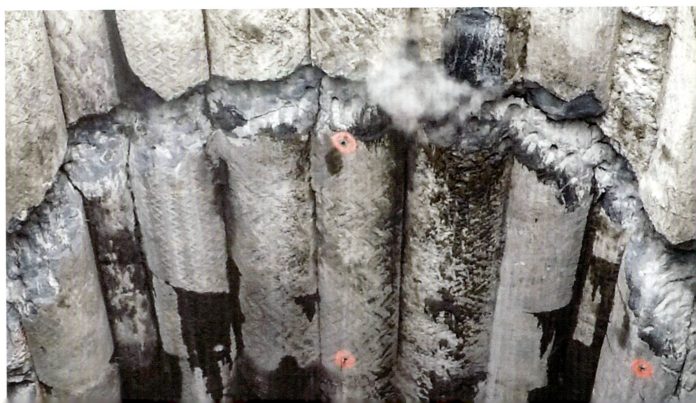

February 19, 2015, 11:00 AM

February 19, 2015, 5:55 PM

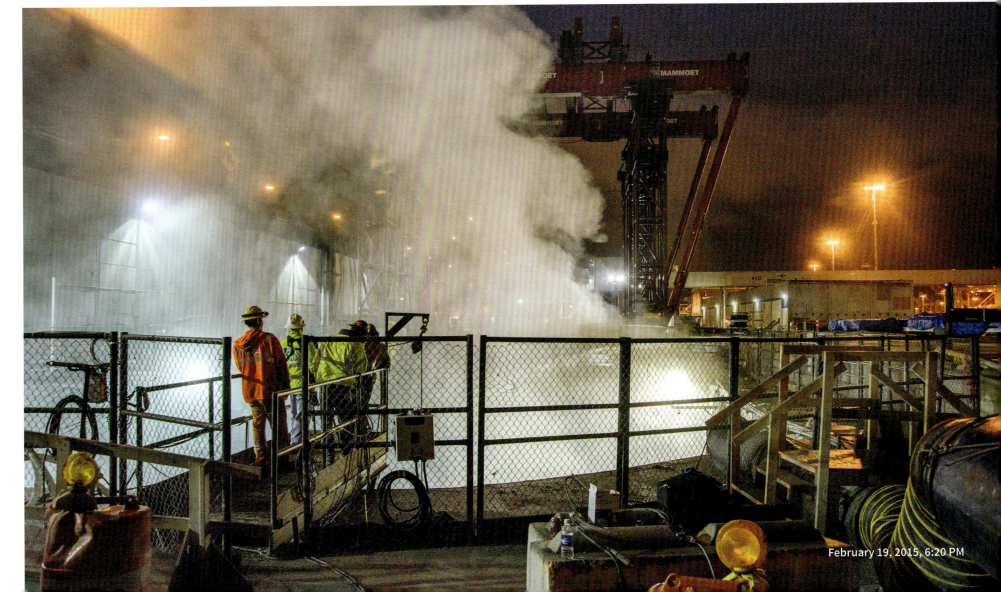

February 19, 2015, 6:20 PM

From high above the Alaskan Way Viaduct and Mammoet's giant cranes (left), to the bottom of the 120 foot Access Shaft, where ironworkers prepare the TBM for the lift up to ground level.

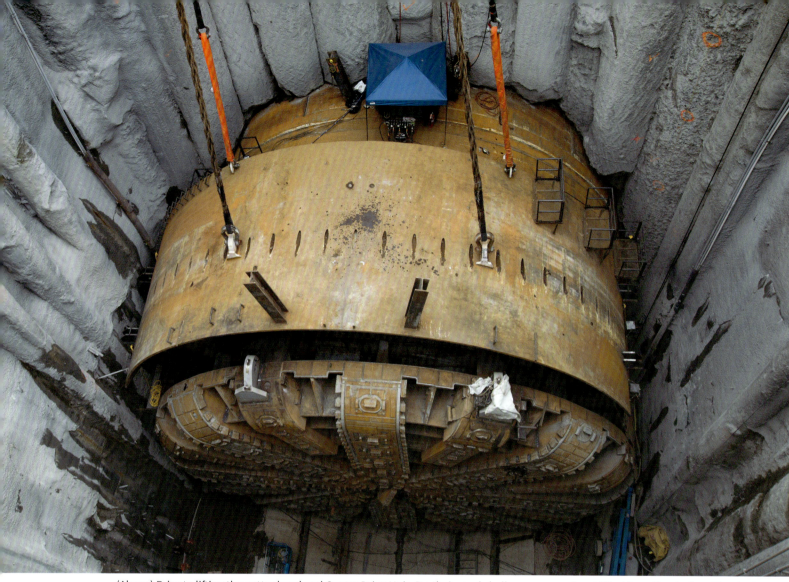

(Above) Prior to lifting the cutter head and Center Drive Unit, Bertha's steel shell was removed and lifted from the shaft on March 19, 2015.
(Opposite) View of Bertha's multi-level interior, following the removal of the Center Drive Unit for repairs.

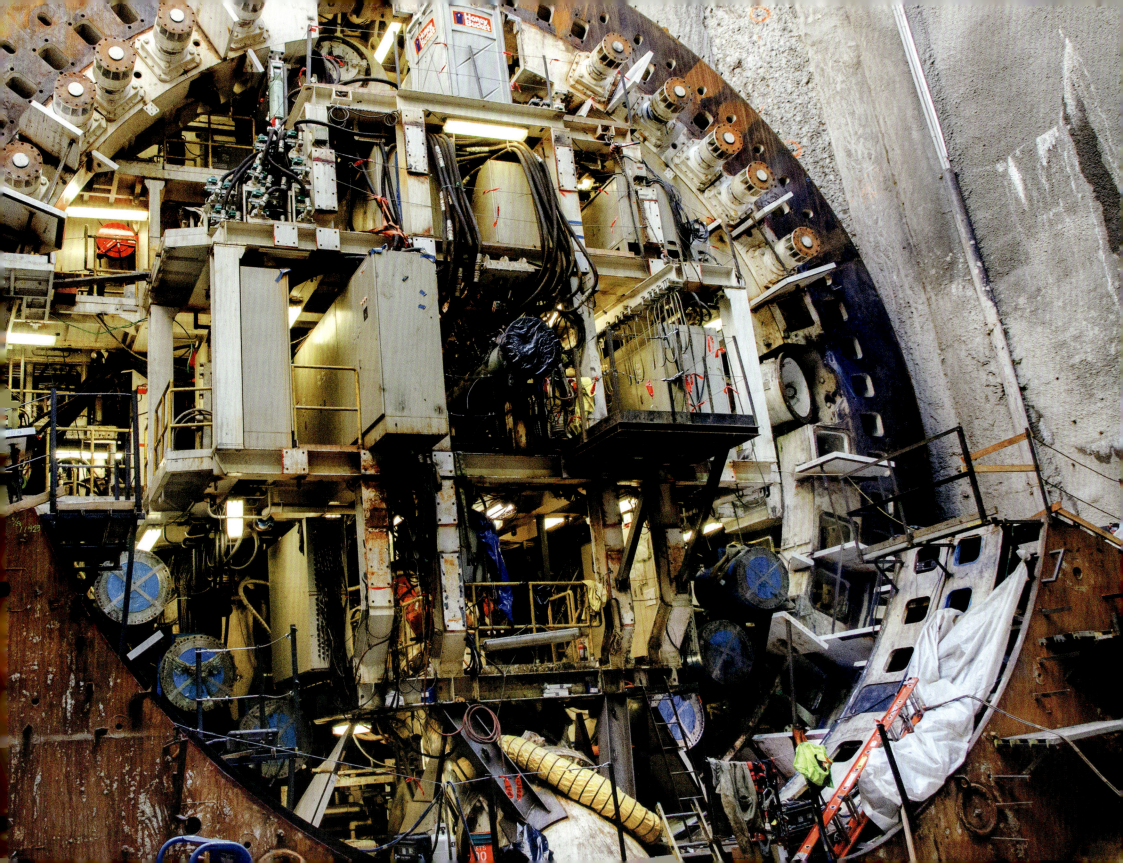

BERTHA RESCUE

BIG SOLUTION FOR A TALL ORDER

The Modular Lift Tower (MLT) was designed and erected by the heavy lift subcontractor, Mammoet, from the Netherlands. The MLT was specifically engineered for this lift and the shaft that it spanned. Sections of the MLT were delivered from countries around the world to assemble the first-ever 'self-balancing' hydraulic lifting tower gantry. Comprised of 48 hydraulic cylinders, the lifting system was based on the principle that the fluid in the hydraulics disperse the weight of the load equally in all directions. This novel solution controlled and stabilized the difficult task of raising the 2,000-ton tunnel boring machine, turning it 90 degrees to a horizontal position, and transporting it to the support frame for repair.

The lifting was done by four bundles of cables that were locked in place with cone wedges and pulled up or let down with hydraulic jacks supporting the cones and the locking mechanism. Nothing moved fast. Every move was carefully planned, rehearsed, and monitored. The day began at 5 AM; the lift required 16 hours. Each step was carried out with methodical precision. By the time the group posed for a photo below the cutter head at 9 PM, it had been a very long day and many of the day shift had already gone home.

(Upper left) Mammoet team members prepare for the big lift atop the Modular Lift Tower Gantry.

(Right) Bertha, the ailing 57.5-foot cutter head, reaches daylight at the top of the Access Shaft. The full heavy-lift event lasted 16 hours.

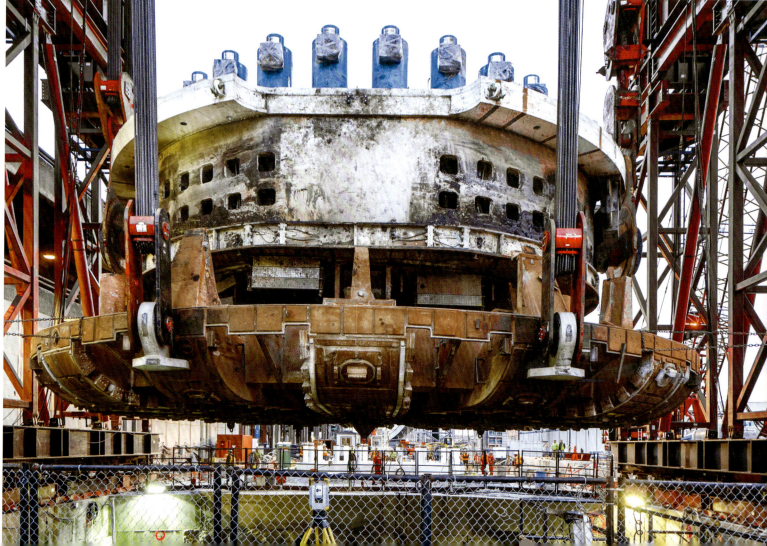

2,000 TONS — 16 HOURS

Mammoet, Hitachi Zosen, and STP crew members celebrate the unprecedented lift to rescue the TBM Bertha from the Access Shaft. March 30, 2015 9:10 PM

BERTHA REPAIR AND RETURN

The replacement seal bearing rings manufactured by Hitachi Zosen arrived at the Port of Seattle on October 31, 2014. In a heavy downpour of rain, these giant steel parts were hoisted from the ship and transported by Gohoffer flatbeds slowly along the pier to their resting spot near the Access Shaft.

It took five months to repair Bertha. These repairs included the cutter head, the seals, the bearing, and the center drive unit. The Hitachi Zosen team of Japanese engineers and technicians were on site working with STP throughout the operations. Several specialty subcontractors worked with the STP mechanics and tunnel workers to complete the repairs and begin the task of reassembly.

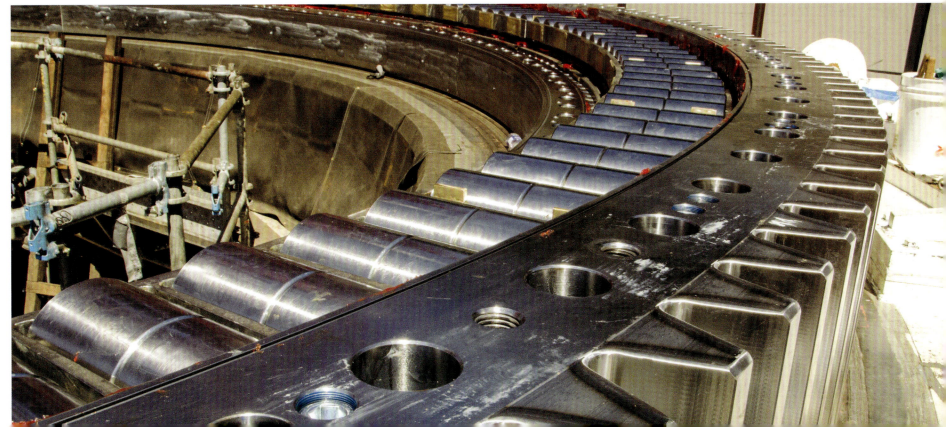

Once the cutter head and drive unit were removed and on the surface, we were able to disassemble the drive unit to see exactly how much damage had been done. The outer bearing seals were completely gone; there was literally nothing left of the seals or their mounts.

This degree of damage was unexpected and much more serious than any of us had imagined. The center can, which mounts to the pressure bulkhead and extends back into the body of the TBM, had severe cracks in its mounting plate and around the connection to the pressure bulkhead. It required removal of the center can, welding up the cracks in the steel mounting plate, and milling the mounting plate to allow the center can to be re-welded to the plate.

This was precision work that is usually done in a shop or manufacturing plant. STP performed this work on site, under a tent—completing major repairs to the cutter head, and completely replacing the seals, the seal ring, the bearing, and the bull gear.

While all of these repairs were going on, we also took the opportunity to beef up the cutters and the cutter head. The cutters were extended outward to give Bertha more space between the solid ground and the excavated soil. We also added additional scrapers at the openings to move more of the excavated soil into the mixing chamber.

The cutter head itself was reinforced, hard-faced, and the openings made larger to improve the flow of the excavated muck. These types of enhancements are not unheard of in the tunnel business, and because of the repair we were able to make these enhancements on a much larger scale.

Gregory Hauser, Deputy Project Manager, Seattle Tunnel Partners

Following five months of repair, the day arrived for Bertha's return to the shaft.

BERTHA RETURN

August 24, 2015

Mammoet, with their innovative Modular Lift Tower, was responsible for lifting and sliding the cutter head and drive assembly over the shaft, turning it vertically, and lowering it precisely into position in front of the TBM body that remained in the shaft. The entire unit was moved forward to be welded in place and make Bertha whole again. This difficult maneuver took a full day and was performed with careful attention and proper placement of the drive unit into the body of the tunnel boring machine.

With the tunnel boring machine repaired and back underground, the Center Drive Unit is reconnected.

(Upper right) Master welder, Kevin Hamilton, working on the top of the five-story tunnel boring machine and (below) a worker standing on the cradle floor.

Bertha's cutter head with hundreds of newly replaced cutter teeth, as the Center Drive Unit clears the rim of the shaft, turning 90 degrees in order to lower down vertically.

Crew members pose with Bertha during the last days of the backfill.

BACKFILL ROCK AND ROLL

Earth Pressure Balance TBMs work by creating a face pressure equal to the water and soil weight trying to enter the machine. After completing the assembly and testing, the TBM was ready for the shaft to be backfilled so that tunneling could resume. The shaft was backfilled with a sand and gravel mixture, which was later compacted so that Bertha had solid ground to mine out of the shaft.

Once the backfill material was ten feet over the top of Bertha, a 20-foot layer of CDF (Controlled Density Fill or light concrete) was added, to give the TBM an impervious layer in order to pressure-up the face to continue to mine forward.

After testing and ensuring that Bertha was ready to mine, she moved forward and out of the shaft. By December 22, 2015 Bertha proved she was ready to continue on her underground journey.

Foreman Jeff Huber, on the tunnel boring machine Bertha, with only the tip of her cutter head visible as the Access Shaft is backfilled. (Photo, courtesy of Will Campbell)

SPOTLIGHT
ON THE JOB

TOPLANDER, WILL CAMPBELL

"I was so excited to get this job. I knew most of the miners from other tunnels. I started out in the hole. A few months later we started mining. We were using the crane to remove the dirt. I was in the hole, signaling to the crane over my phone. The operator was Chuck Campbell and he was running a 150-ton Linkbelt.

Next day I asked Chuck if I should stay up top. He said, "Hell yeah, I like your work so far." I got my rigging and signalman certification. Soon, I was in charge of supplying the machine with anything and everything. I also helped the gantry crane operator with the segments, hooking them up and lowering them into the hole.

After a few months on top side, the machine broke down. It was not looking good. They were laying everyone off, every Friday—I worried I would be next. I never called the boss, I just showed up to work… wow, I made the cut! I would keep working my dream job, on the world's largest tunnel.

I was part of the recovery and repairs. If there was a crane on site, somehow I was part of it, whether it was for the rigging or signaling. Mammoet, the world's largest crane company, arrived to help save the machine. I worked side-by-side with them. I helped assemble and erect their 300- and 600-ton cranes. I had my hands on almost every item that was part of the repairs.

When the cutter was replaced, it was a challenge to backfill the hole. Not only did we have to fill the hole, we had to fill the cutter head up at the same time. We used special sand; it could not just be tossed in. We poured the sand into a big metal funnel with a tube on it. We would move into three different spots, taking sections off as the dirt got higher. At times we would turn the cutter head to get the dirt into it.

After the machine was repaired, I moved back to the beginning of the tunnel and resumed my duties supplying the machine. Many times a day people would call out for things on a mine phone. I was expected to always answer, in case there was an emergency.

I then retired from the laborers and joined the operators. I helped with the concrete on the southbound deck, operating a forklift. I was there for four-and-a-half years. This was a one-of-a-kind job. This was the third tunnel I've been on. I enjoy everything about them. The crews are always tight with each other."

"After a few months on top side, the machine broke down. It was not looking good. They were laying everyone off, every Friday—I worried I would be next. I never called the boss, I just showed up to work… wow, I made the cut! I would keep working my dream job, on the world's largest tunnel."

During Bertha's repair operations, construction advanced on the interior roadways, taking advantage of no mining traffic at the Launch site.

BUILDING THE HIGHWAY WHILE DRIVING THE TUNNEL

While the tunnel was being mined and built, a parallel project was building the interior structures to make the tunnel functional and useful. STP proposed to build the highway itself, the "Interior Structure", while the tunnel was being driven. This had never been attempted in the USA, although Dragados had done so on a project in Spain. This would save time and allow the new SR 99 highway to open sooner.

The process of building the highway

To meet the requirements of WSDOT, STP had to make several concrete pours. Continuous pours were not allowed. Based on the sequence of pouring, 54 feet was determined to be the optimum pour length. The haunches and lower walls were usually placed in facing sequence.

Getting started while the TBM was stopped

With the TBM stopped, and while STP was sinking the shaft to access the TBM, work commenced to build the interior structures. From March through June 2014 workers removed the initial structures in the original Bertha launch area. For this part of the project, it turned out to be fortuitous that Bertha got stuck. Because Bertha was stopped, the Interior Structure concrete crews went through their learning curve without impact from other operations. This made the initial pours and setup much more efficient.

The first concrete placed

Formwork from PERI arrived on site in June 2014. The forms and travelers were assembled and placed in the tunnel. The first corbel pour was on September 2, 2014 and the last corbel was poured on September 22, 2017. (A corbel is a projection jutting out from a wall, as a foundation to support a structure above it. In this case, the corbels support the walls and roadways inside the tunnel.)

Sections were placed in stages. The corbels were the first sections placed, maintaining the 54-foot criteria that had been established. Once enough corbel was built, the lower wall forms were placed, and the walls for the northbound roadway were installed. Setting the forms and making the initial concrete pours took from June 2014 into March 2015.

13 tons of rebar (reinforcing steel, used to tension reinforced concrete) were used in every 54-foot wall panel. Special rebar was used, covered with epoxy to reduce corrosion. CalPortland provided the concrete for the interior structure—enough to build nine Seattle football stadiums.

From April 29, 2016 until the hole-through on April 4, 2017, both tunnel excavation and highway concrete pours were being done simultaneously, with excellent cooperation and coordination of both groups.

 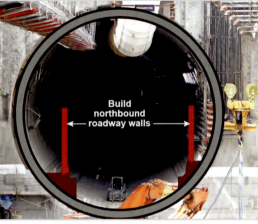 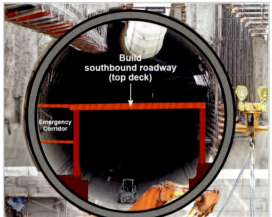 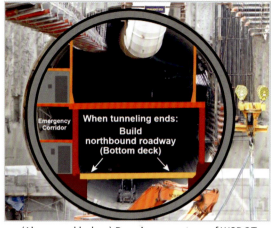

(Above and below) Drawings courtesy of WSDOT

Concrete placement for the upper southbound deck

The upper deck was cast in place. The formwork was left on for a minimum of seven days. Each section of interior concrete cured for 28 days, covered with curing blankets, to reach design strength. The workers strived for the highest quality finish possible because the upper and lower decks would be roadways.

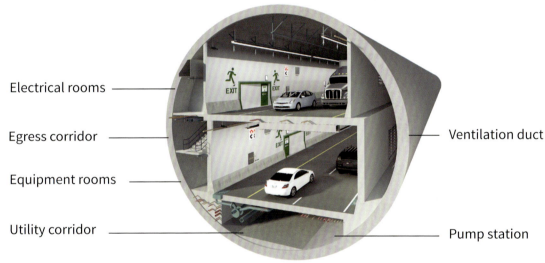

Precast northbound deck

The northbound (lower) deck was made of precast deck panels manufactured by Concrete Technology Corporation, Tacoma, Washington. Delivered to the site on transport vehicles, each panel measured approximately 8 feet long x 29 feet wide x 14 inches thick. These panels were brought into the tunnel and installed as the last phase of the interior structure construction. Panels were post-tensioned in 25-panel sets to make 200-foot sections. A concrete overlay caps the panels and forms the road surface.

Gregory Hauser, Deputy Project Manager, Seattle Tunnel Partners

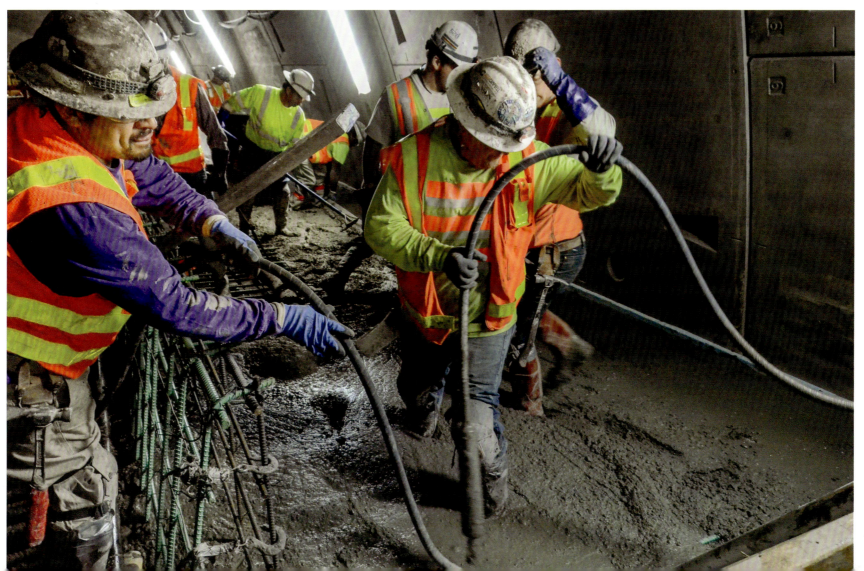

Precast northbound deck installation

CONCRETE

CalPortland supplied 219,538 cubic yards of ready mixed concrete for Seattle's Alaskan Way Viaduct Replacement project. Ready mix concrete is a long- lasting durable material, and a key component of Seattle's built environment. The Seattle Deep Bore Tunnel replaced the Alaskan Way Viaduct that was constructed from ready mixed concrete almost 70 years ago.

With the opening of the Tunnel, the existing Viaduct was removed and recycled. Over 240 million pounds of recycled Viaduct concrete produced in the early 1950's went back into one of the final stages of the Viaduct replacement project—filling the Battery Street Tunnel. The Battery Street Tunnel was a tunnel at the end of the Viaduct. The crushed viaduct concrete was used to fill it in. Crushed concrete from the Viaduct is also being used on other construction projects in Seattle, demonstrating the importance of construction materials as a key component of a circular economy.

In addition to providing ready mix concrete, CalPortland provided 124,477 tons of aggregates used in various applications throughout the construction of the project.

CalPortland was also involved with the material removed from the bored tunnel, the "tunnel spoils". The tunnel spoils went to various sites in Washington State, with over 1.4 million tons of the clean tunnel spoils going to CalPortland's Mats Mats Quarry.

The Mats Mats Quarry began operation in the 1930's and has provided the greater Puget Sound region with quarried material. The mining of the quarry is now nearing completion and the tunnel spoils are being incorporated into the reclamation process at the site.

Scott Nicholson, Vice President / General Manager
Washington Materials Division, CalPortland

(Left) Tunnel "spoils" from the Alaskan Way Viaduct tunnel project are offloaded from a barge, to be used in the reclamation process at CalPortland's Mats Mats Quarry. (Above left) CalPortland at work during a major concrete pour to create the ground-level 'cradle' in the Access Shaft for Bertha's rescue operation. Additional images: concrete work during the building of the tunnel interior corbels and walls that would support the new tunnel road decks. (Opposite, far left, photo courtesy of CalPortland)

INTERIOR TUNNEL WALL

As the tunnel boring machine was being repaired, the tunnel wall segments were simultaneously manufactured in Frederickson, Washington at an off site plant. Delivered by truckloads, they were stored at the main lot above the tunnel launch zone, waiting for the day when mining would resume. Segments were lifted by gantry crane into the launch shaft and placed on the trolley wagon for entry into the tunnel.

1,426 concrete rings were used. Each ring is comprised of 9 segments as shown here plus one smaller keystone piece; 10 segments total per ring. Each of the segments is approximately 17 feet in length and 2-feet thick. The interior of each ring is 52-feet diameter and covers 6.5 linear feet of the tunnel.

WALL SEGMENT PRODUCTION

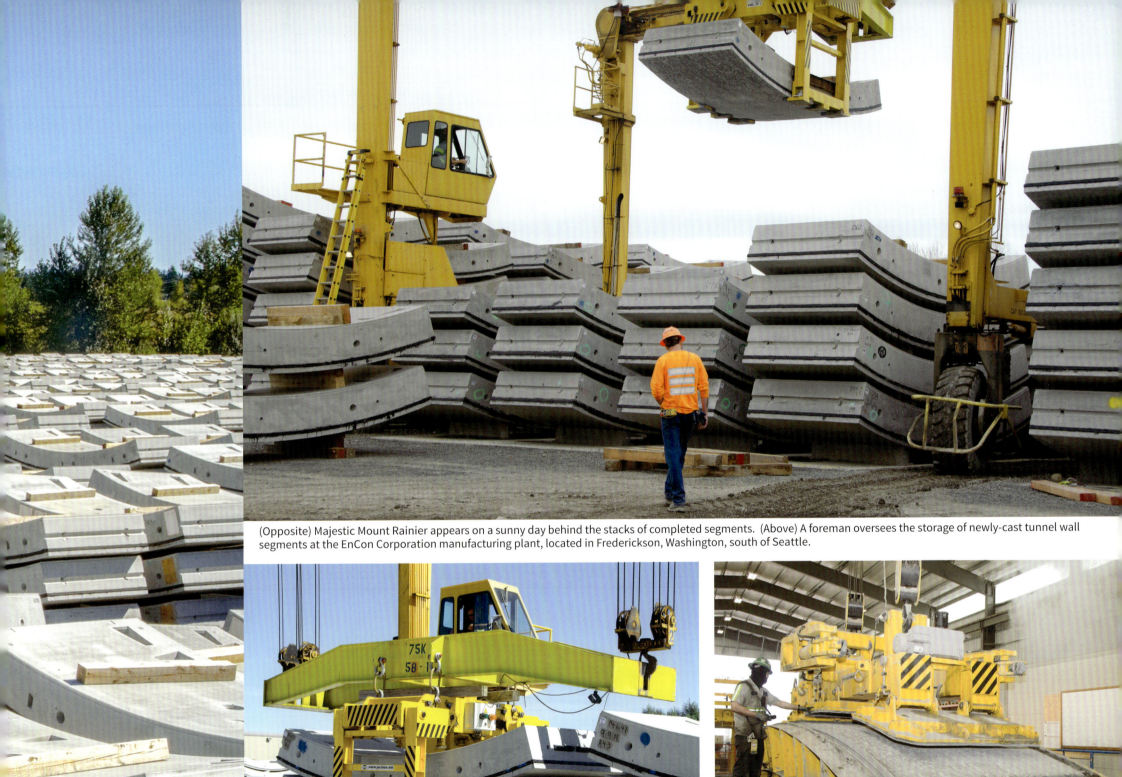

(Opposite) Majestic Mount Rainier appears on a sunny day behind the stacks of completed segments. (Above) A foreman oversees the storage of newly-cast tunnel wall segments at the EnCon Corporation manufacturing plant, located in Frederickson, Washington, south of Seattle.

SPOTLIGHT
ON THE JOB

TEAMWORK: JAMIE WILLARD AND ISMAEL MARTÍNEZ

"One of my jobs was to forklift and move the interior wall segments piece-by-piece. They came in on the truck two at a time, because of their weight. The segments were each numbered. We would unload by number and stack them in the same sequence. Then we would organize each ring by those numbers and stage them in three stacks, making ten segments. The last to load was always the key piece, the one that locks each full ring into place. Then they were lifted onto the gantry, into the tunnel launch shaft, and onto the transport trolley. The 'key' rode into the tunnel on top of the load."

Jamie Willard, Heavy Equipment Operator

Co-workers, Jamie Willard and Ismael Martínez, tunnel launch upper lot

INTERIOR TUNNEL WALL BUILDING OPERATIONS

The tunnel walls were built ring-by-ring, as Bertha moved forward. One ring consists of nine large curved concrete segments and one smaller 'key' piece. Each segment was individually slung into place by the segment erector, a giant mechanical arm run by remote control. Thrust rams slide forward and back to press each segment precisely into the ring before adding the final key piece, which aligned and locked the ring together.

Once a segment was set, the crew bolted them securely in place. After building a ring, the TBM moved forward through the soil and rock, excavating the 'muck', via the screw conveyor, onto the conveyor belt extending behind the machine, and out to the pier to be loaded onto awaiting barges for proper disposal.

Giant thrust rams surround the tunnel wall.

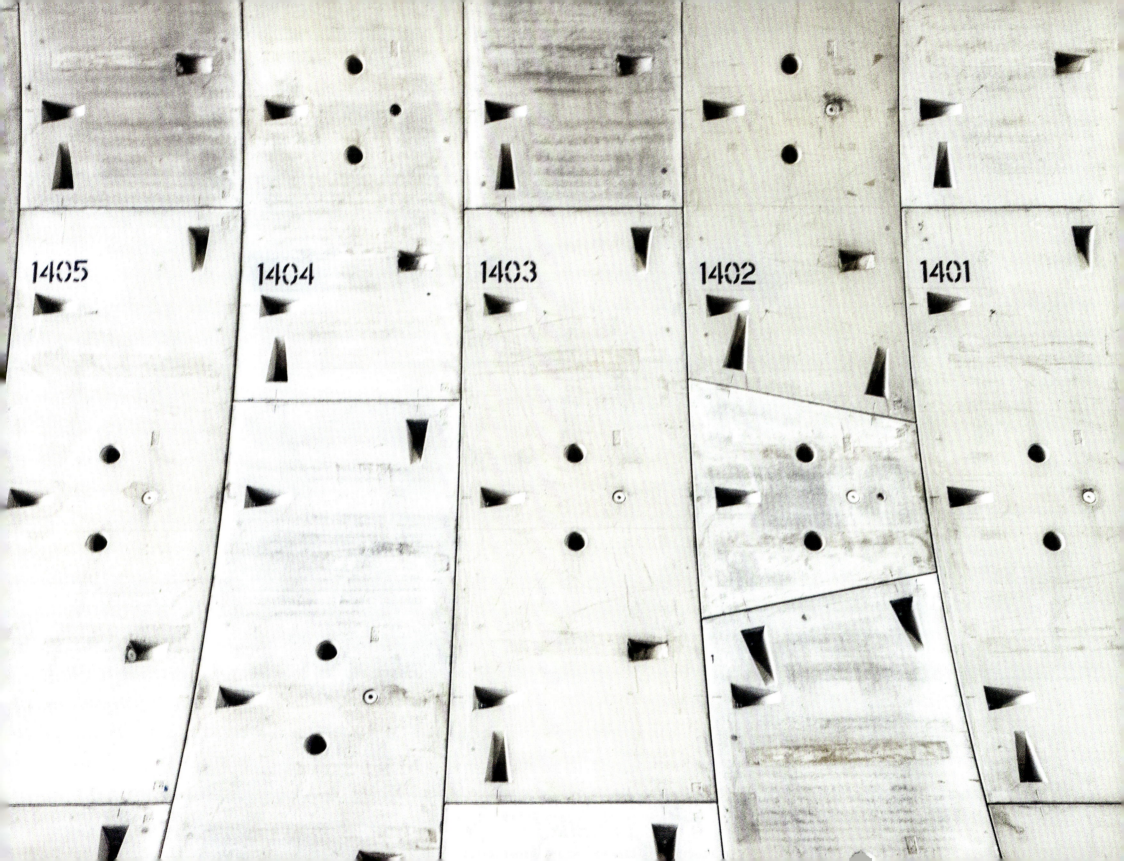

SPOTLIGHT
ON THE JOB

ERECTOR OPERATOR / RING BUILDER, CODY HECK
DAY SHIFT

"I began when they rebuilt the cutter head and they were just about to take off again. When I first started, we were probably building three rings per day shift, and taking about an hour-and-a-half to two hours to build one ring. As time went on, we got more efficient, better, quicker. By the time we were done, it was taking about 26 minutes to build one ring. We were doing about 12 rings per shift. Once we became familiar with the equipment and the tools, where to stand to be most efficient, where to stand to set a segment—everything kind of fell in line.

Tunnel boring machines (TBMs) are sort of similar, but this one was massive. The sheer size and weight was new to just about everyone on that job. On other TBMs the segments are one-foot thick; these were two-feet thick. Most segments are seven to nine feet long and the ones here were 17-feet long. When I first saw the size of the segments I just couldn't believe it. I was like, "Whoa, they're really big!" I was shocked.

We ended up doing all the sides, finishing up with no one injured, which is really nice. It can be a dangerous area with people trying to hurry and go as fast as they can. But we walked away with no major injuries. Yeah, it was a long project, but there were a lot of good people that I wouldn't have had a chance to know; people that I still talk to today. It was definitely a good job for me. I learned a lot; I was thrilled to be on it."

Cody Heck (left) and brother, Mitch Heck, standing at the foot of Bertha.

ERECTOR OPERATOR / RING BUILDER, JUSTYN WORKMAN
NIGHT SHIFT

"I started at Seattle Tunnel Partners in mid-late 2013. They had just launched the machine and were only at ring #3. I was put on the night shift, which I didn't mind because it was better for my 50-mile commute.

I'd been hearing about this project for awhile and about how big it was supposed to be. But I didn't fully understand just how gigantic it was until my first time underground. It was like a five-story building digging sideways underneath Seattle!

I had seven years of experience running vacuum-style erectors. But it took awhile to get comfortable with taking 18 tons over 50 feet in the air.

Our foreman, Edgar Valles, and shifter, Adam Keller, along with the knowledgeable, skilled crew, were the reason we had so much success on night shift. The ability we had to think on-the-fly, overcome any obstacle, and do it as a team, really made it fun to go to work each day. I'm still in contact with a handful of team members.

People may have negative things to say about the tunnel project, but I'm proud to say I was there, that I helped build it, and am happy with what we did. Sure, it took longer than expected, but I wouldn't change the experience, knowledge, and friendships I gained. I'd do it all again."

The Workman family, and Justyn (opposite) setting the 'key piece', the last of the segments in one ring.

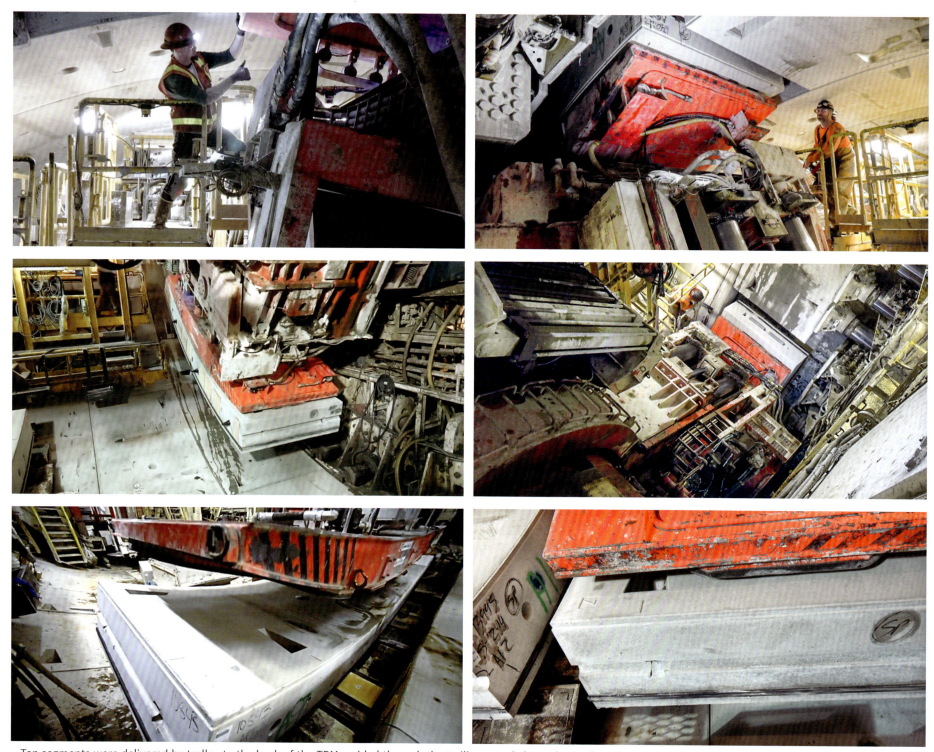

Ten segments were delivered by trolley to the back of the TBM, guided through the trailing gear (a.k.a., 'the can'), and set in sequence on a mechanized rack at ground-level. The Operator ran the segment erector to hoist each segment up into place, forming one ring of the tunnel wall. Photos in this sequence were taken on the last days of Bertha's drive, indicated by segment number 14168, corresponding to the last few rings installed prior to Bertha's exit.

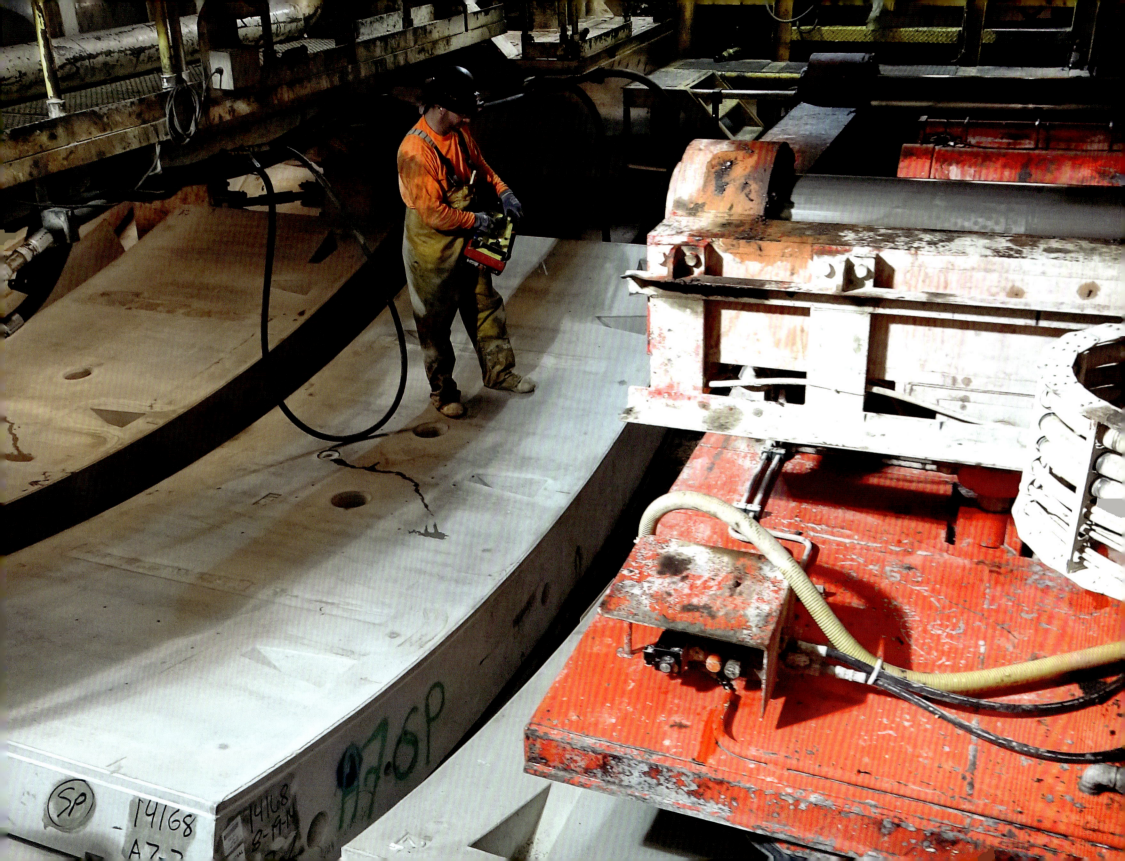

MINING RESUMES

December 22, 2015

Two years had passed since the tunnel boring machine Bertha halted just short of reaching the Alaskan Way Viaduct on December 6, 2013.

During the interlude, the worldwide tunnel industry watched as several events requiring bold, ingenious engineering took place, many for the first time in history. After her rescue, five months of repairs and vigorous testing, Bertha began anew the drive toward her destination at the North Portal.

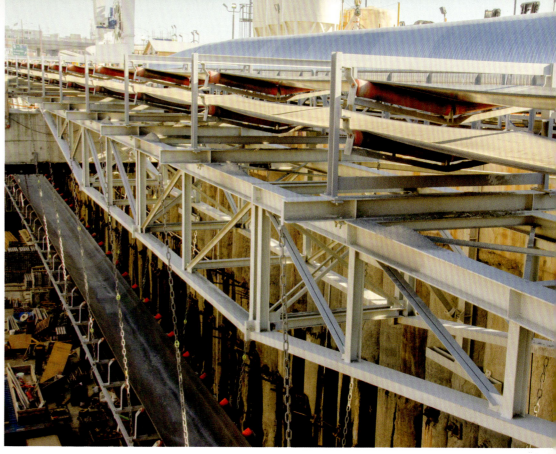

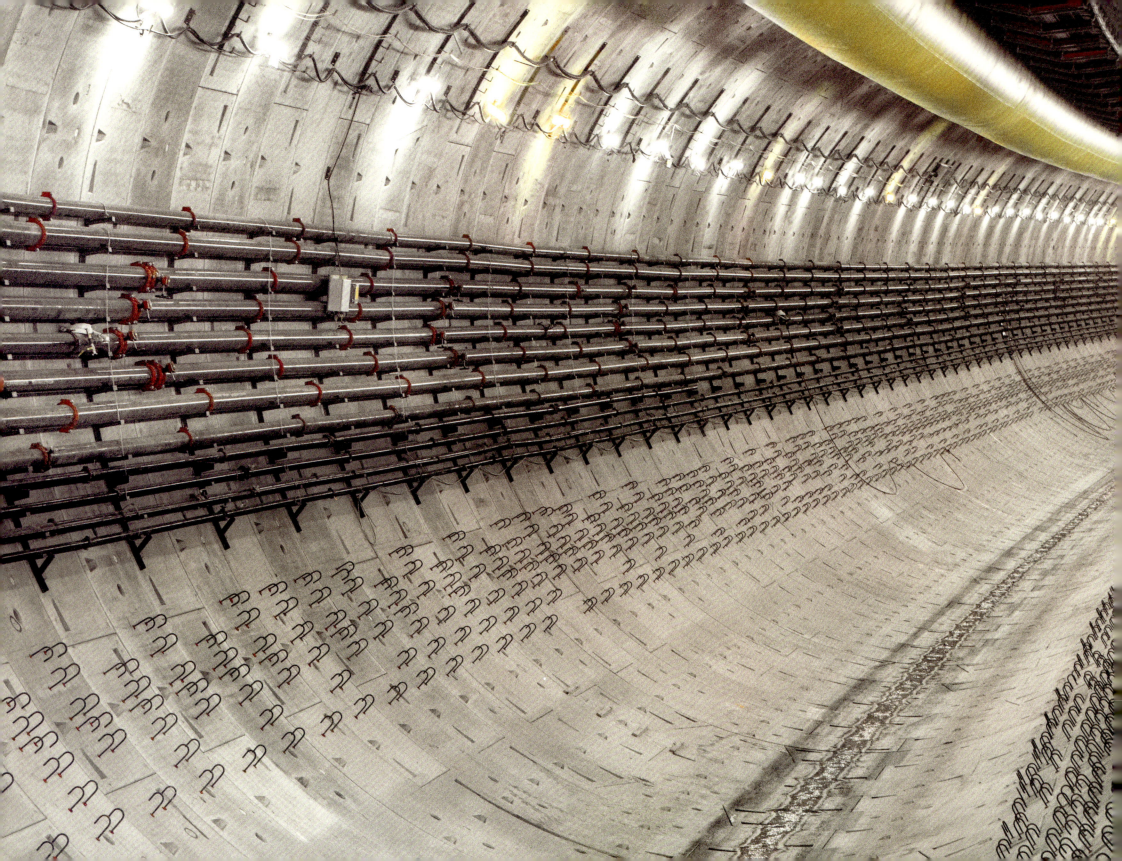

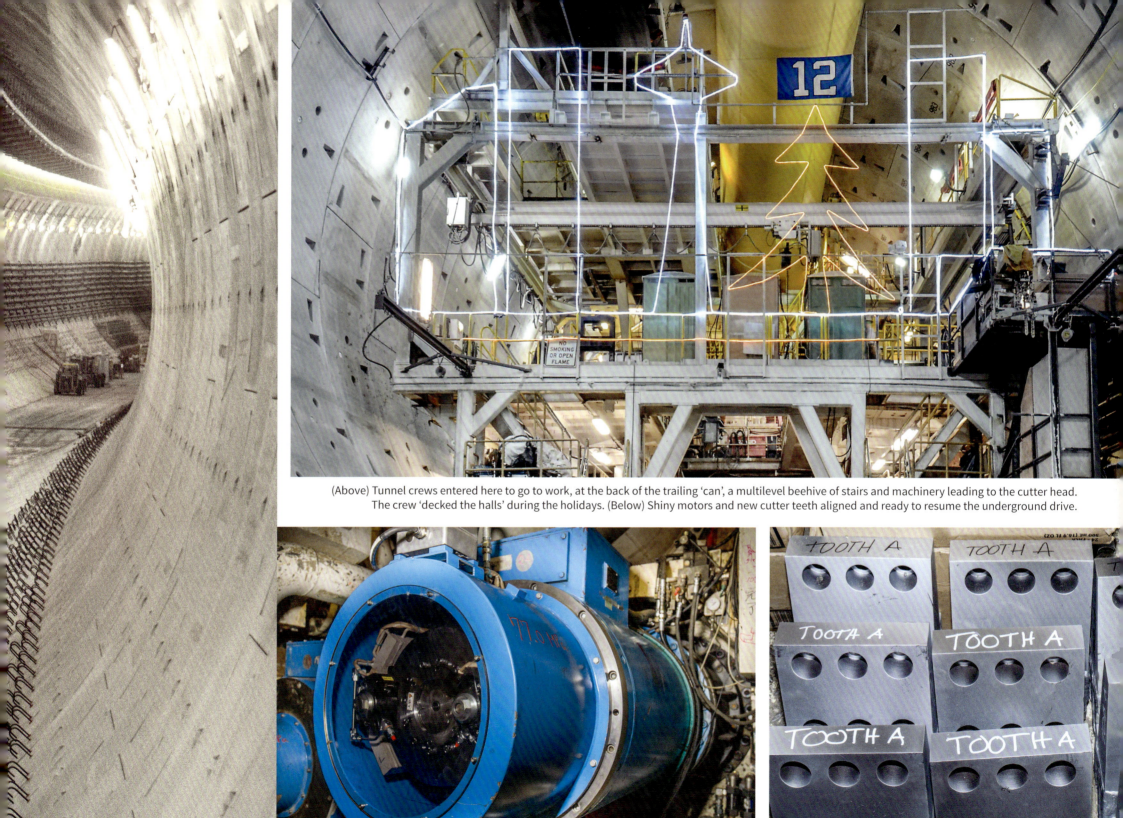

(Above) Tunnel crews entered here to go to work, at the back of the trailing 'can', a multilevel beehive of stairs and machinery leading to the cutter head. The crew 'decked the halls' during the holidays. (Below) Shiny motors and new cutter teeth aligned and ready to resume the underground drive.

SPOTLIGHT
ON THE JOB

COMPRESSED AIR WORKER, CODY HECK

Drew Smith (Ballard Marine), Cody Heck, and Craig McNeil, the dive team ready to enter the chamber

Cody (right) and divers from Ballard Marine riding the trolley in the tunnel to start the day

"We always did a shorter schedule on diving days. I would come in about an hour before my dive time to get a full physical checkout from the doctors on the TBM. We would go over the game plan, what the cutter head looked like inside, what to expect once we got out there, who would be my crew. Once we were prepped and got our okay by the doctors, we went into the first chamber, which would take us down to "depth". That's what they call it, the pressure we were going to work at. It took about a minute. Once we got to depth, we went to the next chamber. We put our harnesses on inside, opened up the door to the cutter head itself, evaluated what was going on, got set up, put up our lights and cameras. Craig and I would go out to clean and change the picks (teeth) on the cutter head itself.

The picks we were changing were about 75-80 pounds each, with six bolts on each one. It was cold and muddy out there. Even though you couldn't see too far below, you knew it was 60 feet down. When something like a piece of rock fell, you could definitely hear it hit the water way down there. It didn't feel so high because it was so dark in there.

Craig and I had a really good system set up—cleaning the windows, the caverns, and the cutter head of all the muck that would come in when we were mining. He would clean one side; I'd clean the other. We'd take the bolts out, remove the pick, send it out to the other chamber, then receive a new pick, line up the bolts, and secure it.

I think we could be down under pressure only about an hour-and-a-half; that's all the work time we had. In an hour-and-a-half I think our best time was completing 17 picks, which is pretty fast, with the weight of them. I had to use the big impact gun to get the bolts out, clean around it, install the new one, get the bolts. It was definitely a go-go-go day. But we wanted that record and we held onto it for the full job. Nobody was able to beat us.

After we were in there for an hour-and-a-half, when our time was up, people outside would notify us. We'd come into the chamber, kick off our harnesses, make sure all our tools were out of the cutter head work area. When you shut the main doors, you pretty much have to strip down to your underwear and get completely clean. They've got hoses inside the compression chambers. There can't be any muck or tools in the compression chamber. So, even though you're wet, you're completely clean. You go into the decompression chamber, dry off with towels, and that's when you begin approximately three hours of decompression time."

Cody and the team working under compressed air inside the cutter head of the tunnel boring machine, replacing cutter 'teeth'. (Center) Compression / decompression chamber

"So we'd get settled in. It was usually a four-man crew sharing a tight area. You wear an oxygen mask. They started with the pressure you were at today, let a little bit out. After about 30 minutes, take your mask off, and you have about five or ten minutes without the mask at a well-adjusted pressure. Then you'd wear the mask again for 30 minutes. Each time they let a little bit of pressure out. After you do that four times, you have a little break at the end before they do what they called "bring you up to the surface". Once you get "to surface", you spend a couple more hours. Finally they open up the main chamber and you crawl through.

When you come out of the chamber, you go directly to the medic's office where there's a nurse and a real doctor to give you a complete physical check: your eyes and ears, your joints, they check everything, and give you snack to get you going. Once you're cleared from the first checkup, you hang tight for another hour. After that hour, you go back in and are checked again just like they did before. Once they release you, you leave the tunnel, and you're off shift until the next morning or next show-up time.

With the prepping and checkups, before and after the dive, I think it turned out to be an eight-hour day for one-and-a-half hour's work. Nothing was unsafe about it; it was all done to protocol. For example, if you got there and had a bit of the flu or a backache, they said, "No, you can't go in." They had men on standby who were healthy and ready to go as backups. There were usually two people from STP and two people from Ballard Marine. Normally the people from Ballard were the ones to hand us the tools, provide the picks and the bolts, replace a tool if it fell down into the pit. They had extras of everything in case we needed a replacement, because if we dropped something, it was gone forever.

I've been a compressed-air diver for many years on different TBMs. When I first started it was a little nerve-racking because I was unfamiliar with what was going on. After a number of years I've gotten more comfortable with it. But I'm never completely at ease because things can go wrong. Things are different in there than the outside world. You have to be a lot more cautious; a lot more aware of your surroundings. Miners want to go as fast as they can to get the most done. But on the other hand, you have to put safety and your tools right there in front. You'd better know exactly what you're working with.

It's definitely a different kind of work. It's not for everybody but I enjoy it. It's grown on me. I like moving quickly and getting stuff done as fast as I can."

Cody Heck, gone fishin'

SPOTLIGHT
ON THE JOB

TUNNEL BORING MACHINE PILOT, JERRY ROBERGE

"I was one of the six tunnel boring machine operators to pilot Bertha. I worked with some solid professionals on the SR 99 replacement tunnel from December 2012 to June 2017 and made some good friends along the way.

I first laid eyes on Bertha in Osaka, Japan during six weeks of inspection and testing before shipment to Seattle. I was blown away by the massive size.

Working with Spanish engineers, electricians, and a lead operator, all of whom had been there the previous year, three American operators and myself dug in to learn all the systems.

Back in Seattle, before the assembly and launch of the machine, I worked as a welder/fabricator preparing for the drive. Once launched, new challenges arose. In order to control earth pressure at the face, it's common to turn the screw conveyor slowly enough to create back pressure. This creates the "balance" in earth pressure balance (EPB) machines, which keeps the face from collapsing.

This machine had a hollow ribbon screw conveyor with no shaft in the middle to stop soupy watery muck from blowing through. We needed good ground conditioning additives injected into the face in order to thicken up the soil to a consistency like pancake batter. It wasn't until after the rescue and repair that two of our engineers made big improvements to ground conditioning."

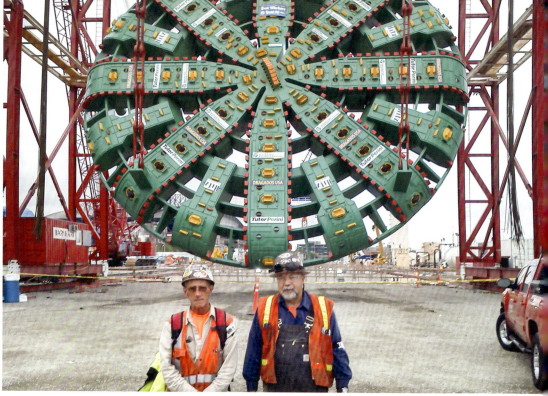

Jerry Roberge (right), and colleague, Mike Allen, with the new cutter head, 'Bertha'

Tunnel Operators, Jerry Roberge (right) and Antonio San Martin Estéban at the helm

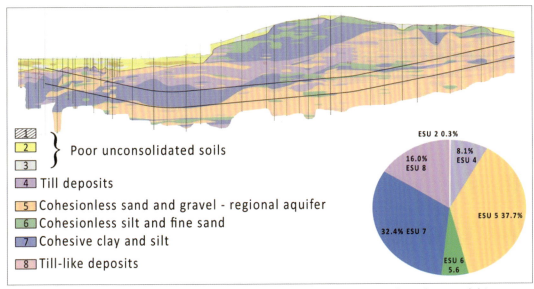

Underground soil conditions along the tunnel drive route

"The geology is an interesting part of any tunnel drive. Core samples of the tunnel alignment indicated a possible stretch of boulders early in the drive. This is the reason for a hollow-ribbon screw conveyor, to be able to pass a three-foot boulder through the center of it. As it turned out, there weren't that many boulders.

Another challenge was information overload. This machine had sensors to monitor 6,000 items that were displayed on six computer screens in the operator's cab. Items like torque, thrust pressures, speeds, flows, amps, volumes, tank levels, and on and on. By the end of a six-foot push your head may explode.

"I have heard that this job can be as stressful as an air traffic controller. I'll agree with that. But, at times, I compare it to sailing. When all conditions are good, the sails are set and trimmed just right, you just cruise along beautifully."

Piloting or steering Bertha was a joy as she responded very well to the controls. The guidance system worked smoothly and we had an excellent tunnel surveyor. We "holed through" right where we were supposed to.

After the breakdown, I spent some time working on the rescue shaft. Once completed, we drove the last few feet, broke through, and pushed forward into the shaft for repairs. After completing repairs, the rest of the drive went reasonably well. So well that a lot of my stress and anxiety disappeared.

We cruised along to the end of the drive with a successful hole through. It was the first time I had witnessed the breakout into the outside shaft via video feed to a monitor in the cab. In days gone by, on the old "open face machines", when you holed through, a big rush of fresh air poured into the machine. Air never tasted so sweet.

All the stress just melts away with a big sigh. Then there are high-fives all around. Everyone scrambles to crawl through the cutter head to be the first ones out to be welcomed by cheers and congrats. In earlier times, you might be welcomed with champagne and fanfare, or a warm beer and a ride in the back of the boss' pick-up truck. Job well done.

Lastly, my hat's off to everyone involved with the project, especially the spouses and families who gave up so much quality time with loved ones due to long hours and hard days."

Off-duty, Jerry is an avid sailor and recently built his own 17' day sailer

CUT AND COVER ZONES

In addition to constructing the tunnel and operations buildings at both ends of the tunnel, STP built concrete "cut-and-cover" tunnel structures at the north and south ends to connect the tunnel to the existing surface streets at the project's entrance and exit.

The concrete cut-and-cover tunnel structures consisted of a base slab, walls, a lower northbound roadway deck, an upper southbound roadway deck, and a roof. As the name implies, rather than boring into the earth, this type of tunnel structure is cut into the earth, built, and then covered over.

To facilitate assembling and launching the Tunnel Boring Machine at the south end of the tunnel, and receiving and disassembling the TBM at the north end, STP excavated and constructed concrete base slabs for the cut-and-cover tunnel structures, creating the Launch Pit and Reception Pit. These were followed by construction of the adjoining cut-and-cover tunnel structures.

After completing the tunnel, STP constructed the walls, lower northbound roadway deck, upper southbound roadway deck, and the roof to complete the cut-and-cover tunnel zones at each end.

Chris Dixon, Project Manager, Seattle Tunnel Partners

2014: Year of the Seahawks Super Bowl victory

CURVE BY CURVE

TUNNEL ALIGNMENT

The alignment of the tunnel was determined by the Washington State Department of Transportation. Considerations included right-of-way easements, minimizing impacts to historic neighborhoods, depth of foundations, and underground structures. The beginning and end of the tunnel were determined by where the tunnel would intersect to the existing SR 99 roadway.

The tunnel was lengthened by STP who proposed a longer tunnel and extended it more than 100 feet further south. This allowed the Launch Shaft to be constructed south of King Street and enabled a gentler grade down to the low point in the tunnel. The final alignment was confirmed by STP to be certain the curve radius was long enough for the Tunnel Boring Machine (TBM) to negotiate and staying within the right-of-way. Also, the curves, both vertical and horizontal, needed to conform to the WSDOT criteria for a highway and the vehicles that would be traveling on it.

Once the general layout of the alignment is established, it is given specific coordinate numbers for Northing and Easting, which are six-digit numbers to four decimal places and very precise. The coordinate numbers are tied into the survey datum for the City and State. These are eventually fed into the computer that establishes the Design Tunnel Alignment or DTA. Once the DTA is established and agreed to by WSDOT, the drawings are prepared, and the coordinate geometry added to every foot along the alignment. Survey points are established in the field and referenced for tying the shaft excavations to actual locations on the ground. The shafts are then laid out and excavated, reliant on these survey points.

After the shaft's excavation, an invert slab is poured. The survey points are transferred to the shaft bottom. The tunnel excavation invert is laid out, either with a dimension to the invert grade, or the invert is established on the head wall of the shaft. These points are also given coordinate geometry numbers which, along with the DTA, are fed into the tunnel guidance system (the computer that directs the TBM). The actual orientation of the TBM in the launch shaft is surveyed, and is also fed into the TBM guidance system. The computer on the TBM now knows its position and orientation. It knows where it is and where it is going.

While mining ahead, the TBM operator can see the actual and design alignment on the screen, steering the TBM to maintain it. Once the ring segments are out of the tail can of the TBM, the tunnel surveyor will start to transfer the control points to the segments. As the TBM continues ahead, the laser and theodolite (surveyor's instrument) will be moved forward. They are always far enough behind the cutter head so that there is no movement from the thrust rams on the segments, but close enough so that the laser is visible to the TBM's sensors.

As the TBM mines, and the tunnel rings are erected in the tail can, the TBM knows where it was when it started a push. It knows what its orientation was when it moved ahead for the next ring. When the TBM has mined far enough to build another ring, the operator stops the forward push. The ring-builder worker measures the last ring position, that is, the gap between the outside of the previous ring and the tail can.

These dimensions are then fed into the computer which knows the geometry of the rings. In order to maintain the DTA (the correct tunnel alignment), the computer tells the crew where the "counter key" is to be located. The counter key is the segment opposite the key segment, which is the last segment piece placed in the new ring. The location of the counter key is the number of the thrust rams that need to be retracted to fit the counter key segment. All of the thrust rams are numbered and everyone in the heading knows which they are and knows the sequence of the rams. The appropriate rams are retracted and the first segment, the counter key, is placed in this opening. The ring is completed by inserting the remainder of the segments, placing the key segment last to lock in the ring. This cycle was repeated every six-and-a-half feet, and the tunnel advanced along the DTA. (Most tunnel rings cover five linear feet; Bertha's covered six-and-a-half feet.) If there is the slightest discrepancy, the computer will generate a correction course to bring the TBM back on grade.

Bertha was so easy to steer that this was not necessary on this project, due both to Bertha and to the experienced crews that we had to staff this tunnel. After repeated pushes, slight errors of inches and feet of deviation accumulate, prompting checks to the survey heading and corrections are made. For this project, the checks were carried out often enough to ensure that the tunnel was never out of the allowed tolerance.

Gregory Hauser, Deputy Project Manager, Seattle Tunnel Partners

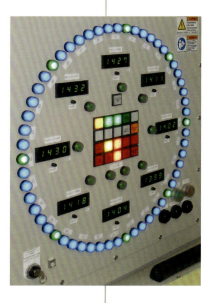

117

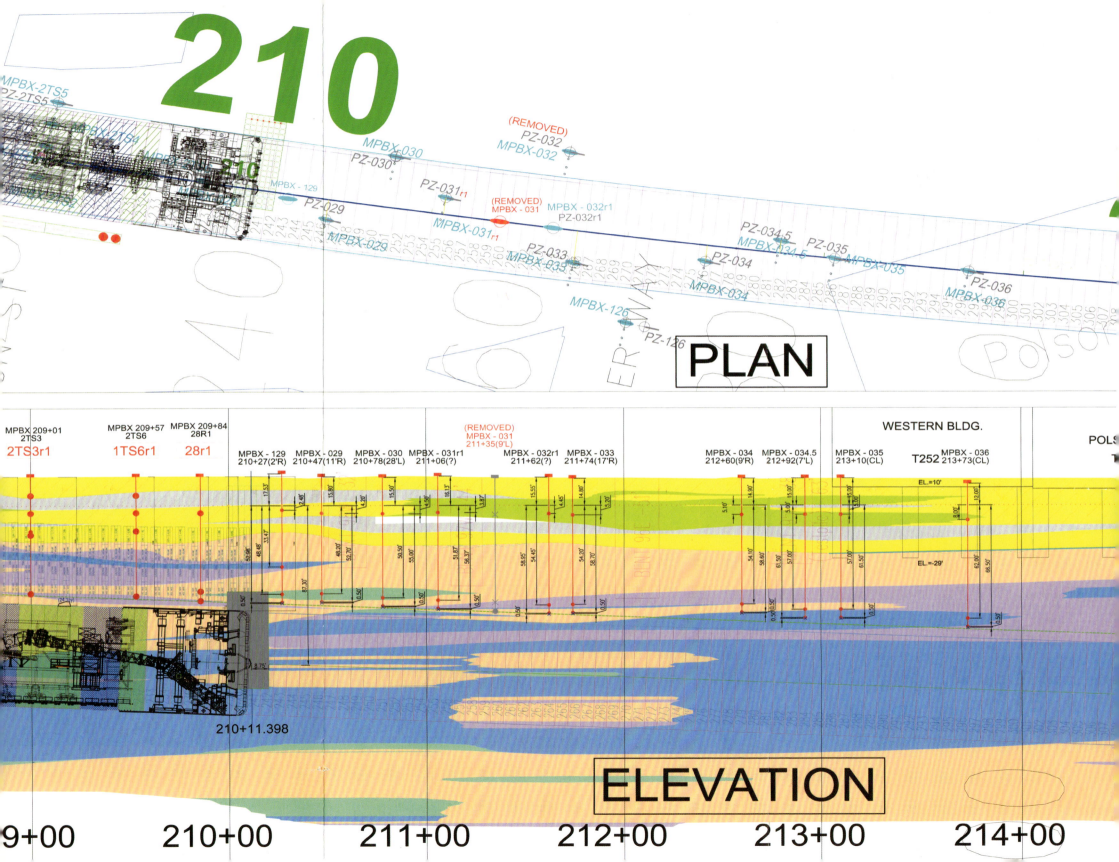

TUNNEL MONITORING

This drawing shows a day's production in both elevation and plan views. The elevation was printed over the geologic profile for the section of the alignment that the TBM had just mined through, and the profile of the ground immediately ahead. The elevation also shows the monitoring devices that were in the area. Bertha appears at the left in both views.

An MPBX (Multi Position Borehole Extensometer) measured the ground movement at several levels (hence, "Multi Position"). The monitoring positions were usually at three levels, but could be at four levels. The lowest was usually about five feet above the planned top of the TBM elevation. The next was usually ten feet above the bottom anchor, and the top was usually ten feet below the surface.

These positions were anchors established at various distances above the TBM. The settlement (or 'heave') was measured at the surface from an established surface elevation. Such renderings were created every day of tunnel excavation and reviewed the following morning before the start of the shift by the Construction Monitoring Task Force (a.k.a. Tunnel Review Committee). This task force consisted of the engineers monitoring the settlement data, the tunnel heading engineers, and the Owners' representatives who were responsible for monitoring the TBM's production and impact on the surface structures.

The MPBX number and tunnel stationing are indicated in the elevation, along with the distance right or left of tunnel centerline. The elevation also references certain structures—here it refers to the Western and Polson Buildings. The plan view shows the TBM's position at the end of the second shift the previous day, the plan locations of the MPBXs, and other monitoring devices. ("PZ" indicates piezometers, which measure the height of the ground water and the pressure in the ground, from the ground water and from the TBM as it passes by.) The plan view also showed the rings and ring numbers installed behind the TBM, but those are not shown in this photo.

The Tunnel Review Committee reviewed the data from the previous day's production, along with data from the TBM relating to soil conditioning, rate of penetration, and torque of the cutter head to understand how the TBM was operated and the results of that operation. In this manner the results could be traced to the varying operation parameters and adjusted as necessary, to prevent settlement and associated damage to surface structures like buildings, roads, and utilities.

For this project, Bertha traveled under the existing AWV and below downtown Seattle, with only negligible settlement at surface during the entire drive. This is truly remarkable for the largest TBM tunnel ever constructed in very difficult soil conditions and a major metropolitan city. The results achieved were accomplished by the combined efforts of the Operators piloting the TBM and the workers who supervised and monitored the excavation of this tunnel. This was a group effort of experienced and knowledgeable tunnel workers, engineers, and managers.

UNDER THE CITY

With tunnel boring back on track, construction continued on several other Project sites, including the North and South Operations Buildings, southern roadways, and the North Portal Exit Shaft. (Left) Worker stands at the front of the TBM interior; crew entering Launch zone stairwell; view of the maze of steep stairs within the trailing gear.

(Right) Worker standing in corridor next to the screw conveyor inside the trailing gear; thrust rams along the top of the tunnel; and the TBM Operator's console in the pilot house.

SOIL TREATMENT AND PROCESSING

(Opposite) Conveyor belt in action, as it turns the sharp corner beyond the launch zone, en route to the Pier for removal. (Center) Master Builders Solutions' on site representative, Jan Babendererde oversees the delivery and hoisting of key chemical components used to break up the 'muck' mined by the TBM.

BREAKING DOWN THE UNDERGROUND

As the tunnel boring machine ground forward, anything in its path entered the giant steel cutter head and into the mixing chamber behind the face of the cutter head. There the soil was mixed and conditioned. It needed to become a homogeneous flowing mixture that could be transported up the screw conveyor. Chemicals were key to this process to break down the 'muck' and condition it. Relying on the optimized use of TBM chemistry, the correct selection of technical soil lubricating foams and conditioners, polymers, and anti-clay agents were used to provide the excavation solution for the soils and varied geological conditions encountered.

The earth beneath Seattle and the waterfront zone is variable and unpredictable. The chemical agents used on the project were adapted and tested to the geology, ensuring the safe advance and maximum efficiency of the TBM. These products helped reduce machine torque and tool abrasion, aided in the reduction of cutter head and screw conveyor clogging, ultimately increasing the excavation and advance rate of Bertha along this famous tunnel drive. All of these chemicals were biodegradable and harmless to the environment. All of the muck transported to the Mats Mats Quarry was tested for environmental contaminates and all passed after extensive testing and documentation.

James Lindsay, Region Head, North America, Master Builders Solutions

SPOTLIGHT
ON THE JOB

WATER TREATMENT FACILITY, ENOCH LISH

"The entire job site was approximately 13 acres, which included the pier, rescue shaft, south operations building, and south SR 99 during the re-routing of roads.

Basically, any water that was generated or fell on site needed to be cleaned to meet what was permitted by the city or the county. The water treatment tank received the water; the water was pumped through; tested in the process to make sure it was clean enough or cleaner than what the permit required; and then we discharged it to the sanitary sewer. We used a plate press to squish the solids out of the water. We used chemicals to adjust and control the Ph to the appropriate level. We used other chemicals to bond the particles together so they would sink to the bottom and the clean water would go out.

This system encompassed any water that was created on site: from the dewatering wells, the drilling operations, the water from the water tower when it needed to be drained a few times. The system was designed to handle all of that, plus the runoff from heavy rain storms. In a heavy storm, there weren't as many chemicals needed, but there were times when our discharge was 530 gallons-a-minute. We set the pumps at 529 gallons-per-minute and that pump didn't turn off for a few days. It ran for 24 hours. I think the longest was about five days straight, in a heavy winter rainstorm.

We used chemicals to break down the soil during the drive. These depended on the soil conditions Bertha encountered, which left foam in the tanks that we had to break down with de-foamer.

The big silver water tank at the end of the lot was a unique feature—it was basically the radiator for Bertha. The water from that tank got pumped all the way to the cutter head through the pipe cylinders strapped to the side of the tunnel wall, continually extending as they mined forward, and then pumped back. You could tell Bertha was running warm if it was steaming out of the tank. If necessary, they drained the tank—all 246,000 gallons—and pumped that to us for cleaning."

Interior pipe cylinders carry water through the tunnel

IMHOFF cones test the settled solids. The clarifier works by slowing the flow of the water down so that the particulates, solids, and pieces of dirt sink to the bottom to test what was in the water.

"I definitely learned a lot, just observing how everything worked. It was the biggest job I had ever been on—eight years of all the different stages, phases, crews. I gained life and work skills being around all that heavy equipment; it was a stepping stone in some ways.

I work with excavators and heavy equipment seven days-a-week now. It's similar in some ways, but a different direction I never thought I'd take and I'm glad I did. I got this job through friendships I made at the tunnel. It was definitely a positive experience. I don't miss the long hours of working 'graveyard', but it was a unique experience I'm proud of. Just the sheer magnitude of the planning, engineering, and coordination that took place on a job like that made it exciting."

246,000-gallon water tank on site

"When I drove through the tunnel for the first time, I thought, 'Wow, I'm going through this with the public now'... but it was over so fast I thought, 'That was it? After eight years, this is it?' I had walked through it so many times that driving it was surprisingly uneventful."

Enoch, with his wife and twins

MOVING THE MUCK

A screw conveyor brought the muck out of the cutter head's mixing chamber, where the muck was under two-to-three Bar pressure or more, depending on ground conditions and depth below ground. Each Bar is 14.5 psi. The pressure dissipated as the muck moved along the screw conveyor, so it was at atmospheric pressure when it was deposited on the conveyor belt mounted on the trailing gear.

The TBM belt carried the muck further down the trailing gear to where it was deposited onto the advancing conveyor belt. The conveyor belt followed Bertha as she mined deeper under the City, feeding out from a storage system on the surface as Bertha moved forward. Miners on the trailing gear erected the structure of the conveyor, and the belt moved forward as Bertha advanced.

When the conveyor belt exited the tunnel, it was contained in the long white box structure visible on these pages. This box buffered the sound and controlled spillage off the conveyor belt. There were transfer points where the conveyor changed direction and the belt moved along through the box until it arrived on the pier, where a gantry extended out over the water and the barges. Once loaded, barges were pulled by Foss Maritime Company tugboats to the Mats Mats Quarry, owned by the CalPortland. In addition to safe advance and maximum efficiency of the TBM, safe environmental and cost-effective disposal of the excavated soil, and occasional re-use of the muck, were important. All soil conditioning agents and processes were approved by STP and cleaned back out of the soil and water.

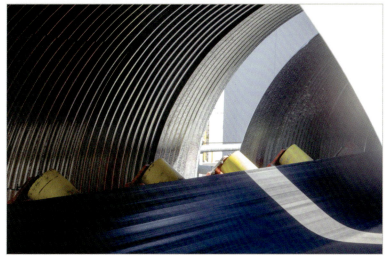

MIGHTY TUGS FOR THE LONG HAUL

With 3000 miles of shoreline and waterways accessing the Pacific Ocean, the maritime industry has defined the Pacific Northwest for millennia. The Strait of Juan de Fuca and Puget Sound are steeped in the lore of great shipping and seagoing vessels from ancient ocean-going canoes, to tugboats, ferries, fishing rigs, freighters, and cruise ships.

Founded in 1889, Norwegian immigrants Thea and Andrew Foss began with a rowboat business in Tacoma, Washington. Foss Maritime is now the largest and most diverse fleet of tugboats on the West Coast and beyond, with global reach. Fitting their solid reputation for tackling demanding assignments, Foss Maritime was chosen by Seattle Tunnel Partners to transport the tunnel "muck" drilled by Bertha from the Port of Seattle's Pier 46 across Puget Sound to Mats Mats quarry near Port Ludlow.

STP required three Foss tugs and four barges to be chartered for the duration of the project, with Foss linehandlers securing the equipment to the pier under the conveyor system built across Alaskan Way. Environmental concerns mandated the muck be transported to the quarry, via barge, versa truck transport to a landfill, due its acidic/PH nature. The barges were modified in early 2013 with watertight eight-foot high bin walls so no material could spill into the water during loading, transit, and unloading.

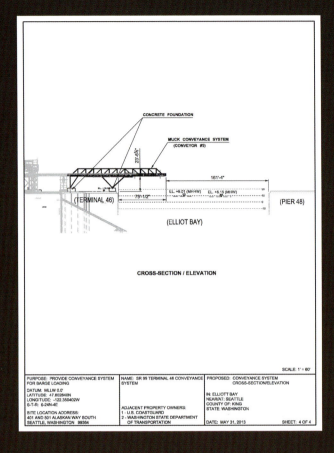

(Top left) Technical graph of the specifications for the loading site at Pier 46, showing the overhang of the muck conveyor belt related to the receiving barge below. Daily tidal changes also had to be factored into the design considerations for how to load the barges.

On October 18, 2013 the first barge load of tunnel muck departed Port of Seattle's Pier 46 for the Mats Mats quarry. After a smooth beginning to the operation, the tunnel boring operation came to an abrupt stop when Bertha was damaged underground in early December 2013, which halted the operation for over 2 years. Marine operations commenced again in early 2016 with the SR 99 Tunnel Project maritime operations ending for Foss in April 2017, after moving 337 barge loads.

In all, approximately 1.2 million tons of muck were safely mined and barged away. Foss crews aboard the tugs SIDNEY FOSS, SIR RICHARD, and PACIFIC KNIGHT worked around the clock, often seven-days-a-week.

Captain John Gore, of the PACIFIC KNIGHT, worked closely with Seattle Tunnel Partners to maintain a constant and efficient pace of operations with three barges and three tugs. During the project, Foss mariners endured many challenges including bitter cold nights, the coldest winter in 32 years, the rainiest February on record, and muck, muck, muck!

This project was an excellent example of the power of teamwork throughout the Foss organization—Labor, legal, commercial, operations, linehandling, billing, accounts receivable, marine personnel with outstanding executive sponsorship—all played a role in the project's success.

Congratulations to all involved for a job well done and the legacy you helped to create in Seattle for generations to come.

Jeff Horst, Vice President of Sales, Foss Maritime

(Above) The SIDNEY FOSS departs Pier 46 with a loaded barge. (Below) Captain John Gore oversees the barge loading, ensuring that each of the barges is stable and safe to sail away.

(Left) Barge docked to unload at the Mats Mats quarry. (Right) Foss CEO John Parrott thanks departing Senior Loadmaster Tom Nixon for a job well done. (Photos and graphics courtesy of Foss Maritime.)

TWENTY-FOUR-SEVEN

LABOR UNIONS AND TRADES

The entire Viaduct Replacement Program, financed with Federal, State, County, City, and Port of Seattle funds, included more than 30 contracts. The largest contract, the SR 99 Tunnel Contract, utilized a PLA (Project Labor Agreement). Any company that worked on this project had to be a signatory to the PLA, meaning they had agree to use union labor even if they were typically a non-union business and had to attend the Pre-Job Union Meeting before starting. In this meeting it would be determined which Union, if any, would claim the work. Union workers would be dispatched to the project depending on the type of work needed. These individuals would then attend the Orientation class, fill out new hire paperwork, and receive badges.

LOCAL 302, INTERNATIONAL UNION OF OPERATING ENGINEERS

The International Union of Operating Engineers 302 was proud to be a part of the historic construction of the Seattle Deep Bore Tunnel Project. Like any large-scale project this one was not without its challenges, but we consider safety the primary metric for success and that all workers return home after work, which was absolutely true for this job with no fatal accidents or major catastrophic incidents.

This was a great job for the women and men of the International Union of Operating Engineers and we were honored to have had the opportunity to work for numerous contractors alongside members of all the other building and construction crafts in the successful completion of one of the largest tunnel projects in the U.S.

Marge Newgent, Field Representative

LOCAL 86, IRONWORKERS UNION

Ironworkers Local 86 supplied a skilled workforce of over 150 journeyman and apprentice ironworkers to more than a dozen signatory union contractors over the course of this monumental project.

Ironworkers participated in all phases of construction from erection of the gantry and support cranes, unloading and hoisting material, and installation of reinforcing, structural, post-tensioning, and ornamental iron. Hundreds of thousands of man hours were worked on the Tunnel, as well as on all of the supporting infrastructure.

We are proud to have played a vital role in the construction of the newest piece of Seattle's transportation system, and the reshaping of our waterfront.

Derek Patches, Business Agent

LOCAL 440, STREET PAVERS AND TUNNEL

Laborers Local 440 involvement in the WSDOT SR 99 Project began with attending council meetings and community group meetings to promote the tunneling concept. We took part in the negotiation of a Project Labor Agreement. Once awarded to the Seattle Tunnel Partners (STP), we began working with their team to detail the processes to be utilized.

I was fortunate to be a part of the process and truly honored to have represented all the men and women laborers within our craft who did the traffic control, warehouse management, seismic monitoring and settling, well drilling, pipe layers, concrete work, tunnel hands (miners), compressed air workers (in tunnel), bull gang, topside support, conveyor systems, finish grade, landscaping, and paving.

We provided 250+ workers at the peak, who gave their all, often seven-days-per-week, enduring the long hours and physically demanding work to produce a quality product, which one can now experience when driving through the new tunnel.

Laborers Local 440 has since been merged into Local 242. All those same workers are still working hard each day completing other projects in the region.
May they always stay safe!

Michelle Helmholz, Field Agent

LOCAL 174, DRIVERS

Teamsters Local 174 was chartered in 1909, and represents 8,600 hardworking men and women primarily in King County. Our members are mostly drivers, though we represent workers in nearly every job classification—from aircraft fuelers to warehouse workers and everything in between. We believe in the power of working people standing together to build a better life, and we are champions in the fight for economic and social justice not just for our members, but for our communities.

This tunnel could not have been built without the hard work done by Teamster drivers. Our members were responsible for transporting workers in every job classification from their parking facilities to the job sites and back again, day in and day out. Our members operated water trucks throughout the job site to keep the dust down and allow other workers to perform their jobs safely, and operated sweeper trucks to keep the area clean. All the concrete poured in that tunnel, along with the secant pile wall installed to remove Bertha's cutter head, came from trucks operated by Teamsters Local 174 members. The precast concrete segments that were used to construct the tunnel were delivered by Teamsters. Sand, gravel, and any other necessary materials were brought to the site by Teamsters, and then some of the debris and dirt were removed from the site on dump trucks driven by Teamsters. Our members were truly instrumental in accomplishing some of the dirtiest work in the project.

On any given day, there would be one-to-two dozen Teamsters working on the tunnel. All told, around 100 Teamsters Local 174 members participated in building the historic tunnel.

Rick Hicks, Secretary-Treasurer

Formwork and foundation building for tunnel interior walls

PACIFIC NORTHWEST REGIONAL COUNCIL OF CARPENTERS

Members of the Pacific Northwest Regional Council of Carpenters are proud to have worked on the Seattle Tunnel Project from one end to the other, over the entire five-year life of this ambitious undertaking.

Piledrivers from Piledrivers, Bridge, Dock, and Wharf Builders Local Union 196 were on site for the excavation and pile driving work. Union carpenters from Locals 30 (Renton), 70 (Mount Vernon), 129 (Lacey), and 816 (Renton) built supporting infrastructure and forms for the precast segments placed by the Hitachi Zosen Tunnel Boring Machine. Union carpenters also built decks, vertical walls, doorways, and pony walls. Union interior systems carpenters from Local 41 performed the metal stud framing and drywall in the control tower interiors at either end of the two-mile tunnel.

At the peak of activity on the Seattle Tunnel Project, nearly 150 Union carpenters were on site. Although it was sometimes a difficult and demanding project, it also created opportunities for innovation and collaboration with the other skilled trades and provided a unique and challenging learning environment for our apprentices.

While the world watched, carpenters and other union tradesmen and tradeswomen worked together to complete this landmark project.

Ryan Hyke, Regional Manager

Structural carpentry on the exterior curve of the tunnel launch opening

UPCMIA LOCAL 528, PLASTERERS AND CEMENT MASONS UNION

Local 528, Plasterers and Cement Masons, had several signatory contractors who performed many scopes of work on the SR 99 Deep Bore Tunnel Project.

Seattle Tunnel Partners were averaging 30 Cement Masons throughout the duration of the project. Clayton Coatings had about 15 Plasterers who performed the lathing and fireproofing. Other companies who were performing work on this project and employing Cement Masons were FD Thomas, Superior Gunite, Acme Concrete Paving, Contech Services, and Gary Merlino Construction.

Local 528 was able to supply effective manpower for the duration of this unique, four-year project and our members are proud to have been part of it.

Marilyn Kennedy, Recording Secretary

Hundreds of skilled trades were involved in fulfilling the tasks required daily to meet the needs of the SR 99 Tunnel. Six major work zones buzzed with multiple activities around the clock. As Master Mechanic Roger Williams put it, "The tunnel doesn't sleep". Here he answers an early call to wire a key component for his team that would arrive in a few hours.

Roger Williams, Master Mechanic for Malcolm Drilling, working at the Access Shaft excavation site.

MOVING ON UP
PERLA GARCÍA,
CARPENTER APPRENTICE TO SURVEYOR

"I started as a carpenter apprentice in 2012. We started by building forms in the launch pit at the South Portal and then the South Operations building. When I started that job, I always wanted to grow. As time went by, we became like a family. Two or three years into the project I had an opportunity to help out the survey team. I joined the survey department, laying out walls in the launch pit, the corbels, all the interior structures.

I helped the survey department lay out the tunnel, inside and out, including the northbound walls and the southbound deck. It was a great experience. It wasn't about work; it was more about the family of workers. We just had one goal and that was finishing—drilling through and seeing the light at the end of the tunnel.

This was a once-in-a-lifetime opportunity. You had to put everything else aside. I met wonderful people who have been doing this work for a lot of years. They have a lot of experience. I saw how they treated other people, which made me want to achieve this big goal, this project. We celebrated every time we would accomplish the last part—every time we poured the cement for the last section, the final corbel pours—we celebrated. We brought food and shared with the workers. It was more like a friendship; it wasn't like, "Oh, I must go to work". It wasn't repetitive. We still keep in touch with other co-workers and I get the same feedback that yes, it was a once-in-a-lifetime opportunity.

I got this job by sending my resume to HR. I had an interview with the carpenter foreman as an apprentice. It was a challenge working in the tunnel because I'm not used to working in enclosed spaces. There was no phone reception, so you had to talk to people and share stories. That's how you became more connected to everyone. Everything was interesting about this work. For example, this construction was not at 90° angles, everything was curved and changing.

I transferred on to be a surveyor. Now I could see the whole picture. With the cement pour sequences I always had to be a day ahead of the concrete. I had to stay ahead of about 90 carpenters.

I think it was unique because it's the biggest tunnel; a massive project. We were all thrilled to be a part of it. Driving through the tunnel, I remember everything: the precast southbound deck, the utilities, the egress, the North and South buildings, the 'Paradise island,' and south roadways like Royal Brougham… I don't have words to describe how wonderful this project was."

"When you have fun with your co-workers, anything is possible."

Perla, five years into her career path, on the surveyor crew. Fall, 2017

SPOTLIGHT
ON THE JOB

SENIOR SITE ADMINISTRATOR, LISA MILLER

"As a Site Administrator (from May 2012 to August 2018), I was a liaison between the corporate offices and the construction site. I coded and processed invoices, reviewed time sheets, distributed payroll, submitted new hire requests and layoffs to all union disciplines, processed that paperwork, and ordered supplies for both South and North portals. I assisted employees on site with any HR issues or requests, distributed mail, red-lined drawings with new updates, maintained and tracked some of the Motorola radios used on site. I was busy!

The most challenging part of my job was keeping the processes organized and on time for time sheets, invoicing, and hiring of union workers. Compared to my previous jobs, this was a high-visibility position.

The most interesting and satisfying parts of my job were the relationships I developed with many union workers. Now that the tunnel is open, I mostly remember the wonderful friendships I had. I wanted to make their work lives as easy as I could. I went the extra mile to help them, responding to requests from coffee supplies to payroll. When I first interviewed for the job, I was so ignorant about how large a project this was. I soon discovered that I was a part of something really big! I was often referred to as "the glue that stuck things together". I was the sixth person hired for this position. I guess the others couldn't handle the construction environment and quit. Everyone I worked with was pretty great; I never really had any issues. I was there to help and feel like I did a pretty good job.

My favorite times were going into the tunnel—watching the sections being placed; what an achievement! Another fun time was being lowered into the rescue pit—the guys working in that pit were so muddy from all the power spraying they were doing. They all worked so hard and sometimes it was so dangerous; I was proud of all of them and proud to be a part of it, working with the best in the business.

"I don't know that the public can really appreciate how dangerous this project was and how hard all the work was."

How deep is your love?

During this time on the project, my boyfriend of ten years and I decided to get married. We wanted a ceremony that was really different, yet simple. We were having difficulty coming up with an idea. My older brother suggested we get married in the tunnel! I thought, what a cool idea. I ran it past my sweetie and guess what?—on September 18th, 2015 we got married at the south entrance (after getting approval from my boss and the Safety Manager). It was so much fun and something I will never forget. My mom, my best friend Melinda, and I were lowered 90 feet to the bottom, in a "man cage". Our hard hats and safety glasses were trimmed in pearls and lace. My sweetie met us at the bottom, having just finished up a tunnel tour with his brother and sister-in-law. A co-worker, who became an ordained minister just for us, performed the ceremony. The cutter head was under repair during this time. There were a lot of tours going on, so it was a perfect time to do this. It was truly a special day."

RIGHT HAND MAN

CHRIS LUCAS ROSCOE,
SKILLED LABORER

"I was living in California, when Jake Chopic extended me a job offer on the TBM Bertha. Not long after that, I relocated back home to Washington State.

I started on Bertha in October 2014. Through the years on different tunnel jobs, I have been cross-trained on just about everything. Therefore, when there was a demand for support in one area of the machine, I was able to shift over and fall in line to provide the added support. Anything from guiding and off-loading segment trucks, adding utility pipes, adding conveyor belt brackets, adding wall brackets, adding ventilation bag line, off-loading segments with the segment crane, greasing segments, operating the segment feeder, changing cutter head tools, bolting up ring segments, to operating the erector building rings—I was your guy.

I assisted with limping Bertha into the Access Shaft where we disassembled, rebuilt, reinforced, and re-installed her. I was down in the tunnel and in the hole for most of this process—strengthening her "skeleton," so to speak, with steel re-enforcement plates and beams.

Once the long, painfully meticulous rebuild was complete, Bertha was then back off and mining. During that time, Bertha was the largest mining TBM in the world; vast and complex. Bertha did not come without her issues, though.

My hat goes off to Jake Chopic, who, as a "Walking Boss", was in one of the most pivotal roles throughout the project. He was challenged with the daunting task of manifesting the wishes of the upper management into a reality down under Seattle, by way of man and machine. He did a wonderful job of motivating and allocating his crew so that Bertha would go on to mine ahead of the forecasted production rate. This high level of production continued all the way through the remainder of the project, until Bertha finally broke through, completing the SR 99 tunnel under Seattle—a task some considered to be impossible.

After we holed out the TBM, I continued on with the project; disassembling and removing the utility pipes and the conveyor system from inside the tunnel, until around July 2017."

"From working on this tunnel, I learned that even in the face of negativity, doubt, and resistance from forces outside one's control, you can accomplish a big goal when supported by hard work, sacrifice, and dedication."

Chris delivering new cutter teeth through the corridor to the front for replacement.

Chris is an avid hiker, here at Summit Lake, WA with his sister, Andrea

A FAMILY AFFAIR

SHAWN OVERBY,
CARPENTER TO FOREMAN, NORTH PORTAL

"Working on the tunnel was not by accident for me. It was a long time coming. My father, Steve Overby, has been in the tunnel industry since the early 1980's. He helped me get my first tunnel job after the Marine Corps, in Minneapolis-St. Paul, MN. Since then, I worked on four tunnel jobs around the country, most recently the Capitol Hill Light Rail tunnel and station. All eyes were on the SR 99 tunnel, waiting for it to kick off.

In 2012, my stepmom, Robin Overby, landed a job working for Tutor Perini on SR 99. Soon after, my brother, Matt Overby, and I were hired by STP. We all went our own ways within the company. Robin went to Safety, Matt to the TBM, and I went to the North Portal to work as a carpenter for Tim Miller and Nate Burch. In 2013, I started out as a Journeyman Carpenter and moved my way up to become Superintendent Nate Burch's right-hand man for the carpenters and subcontractors. I oversaw subcontractors, making sure the subs were staying on schedule and moving forward.

In 2017, my father, Steve Overby, was working with Frontier Kemper and ended up on the job dismantling Bertha. Now it was a full-on family affair with four family members working on the same project. In 2018 my job made the transition into overseeing the commission and turnover of the North Portal building to WSDOT. This is the job where I honed my skills, allowing me to move from the field to the office.

"The fun part about big jobs like this is the organized chaos that it takes to accomplish projects of this size. Overtime comes with a schedule that gives little or no time for error, so you must dig in and push forward to finish."

For example, I was the foreman for the carpenters setting 50' wall sections. We would set one side and then wait for rebar and the installation of MEP (mechanical, electrical, plumbing). After the one-sided wall was signed off with the correct rebar and MEP, we were able to close the wall and prep for the concrete pour.

One day, I got the crew ready to close, planning a three-hour deadline to get out by 5 PM. Up in the crow's nest, birddogging us setting the first panel, were three Superintendents: Joel Burch, Keith Burch, and Nate Burch. Of course, the pressure was on to perform well. We flew the first closing panel down, to start three hours of go-go-go. The tapper tie holes were not lining up. After further investigation, I realized I had set the back-panel upside down. By now I couldn't ignore the yelling from the crow's nest, so I headed up and got reamed by three guys like it was boot camp again. The whole crew just witnessed me get chewed up and spit out, so I went back down with a smile and commenced to getting the work done. The crew saved me that day! We ended up leaving at 10 PM, five hours after we planned on leaving and doing five times as much work just to finish. I cost the company a lot of overtime hours, but the outstanding, hard-working crew did not skip a beat and did not miss the concrete pour."

(Left) Shawn, late night at the North Portal tunnel interior, and (above) the Overby family.

AMAZING JOURNEY

MARISA RODDICK,
LABORER TO SAFETY MANAGEMENT

"I had an amazing journey at STP. I started as boots on the ground—and I use that term loosely, because the ground was mud. Some days the mud was knee deep. I was on the wheel wash seven days-a-week with Derrick Jones for 18 months. It was a daily routine of cleaning rumble strips, helping truckers remove rocks from their duallys, poking out the holes in the wheel wash for optimal performance. It could be tricky because people would walk in front of a sensor and set it off, while I was standing in the middle of it, possibly soaking me! We would flush the system fully at least once-a-week, depending on the turbidity. I also worked with the Vac trucks to remove the mud around the job site.

Marisa Roddick (left) during a concrete pour on site

We didn't have a break area when I started. If we were lucky, the water truck would be parked at the wheel wash, and we could stay dry on break. I remember one day, in front of the South Operations Building excavation, it was so cold my water bottle was freezing from the outside in. I just kept sweeping to stay warm. Eventually Derrick built a pretty swag shack. It was so nice to be able to get out of the rain.

Then I transferred to the concrete crew, where I spent two years. I ran tail for the concrete vibrator when we were pouring. We were running rock drills 12 hours-a-day for weeks at a time. We did the same thing with chipping guns, getting the walls of the shaft ready for layout. I became responsible for all the cure blankets. After a concrete pour, the Finishers would lay blankets, and I would water them daily to cure the concrete.

Next I spent three years in the Safety Office as a safety representative and worked my way up to Manager of Safety and Health on the project. My first assignment in the Safety Office was to identify all the chemicals used on site and create an online matrix for easy reference. I'm not really "techie", but YouTube helped a lot on learning how to paste web links into Excel. After I finished cataloging safety data sheets, I was trained to perform daily air monitoring throughout the tunnel. As Bertha journeyed forward, my walk got longer and longer.

Marisa Roddick, 'brassing in' to go down into the tunnel

I became an OSHA-authorized outreach trainer and a first aid trainer. Then I took over training at STP. The training schedule changed a few times, but at its peak I was training three days-a-week. I spent four years on the Tunnel Rescue Team. We ran drills and training once-a-month.

I met so many awesome men and women that work hard every day to build our city. They all made going to work feel like going to hang with friends. It wasn't always easy, but teamwork made it easier. I built relationships that I hope will last a lifetime. Now I am a Safety Manager at another big job in town. Words cannot express how grateful I am for every opportunity I was given at Seattle Tunnel Partners."

Marisa takes a break

"I had an amazing journey with Seattle Tunnel Partners. I started as boots on the ground—and I use that term loosely, because the ground was mud. Some days the mud was knee deep."

SITE OPERATIONS BUILDINGS

SOUTH PORTAL

The South Operations Building is located above the SR 99 tunnel southern entry and exit, adjacent to the industrial district and sports stadiums.

NORTH PORTAL

The North Operations Building is located two miles north, at the location where Bertha completed the underground drive, at Harrison Street, near the Space Needle.

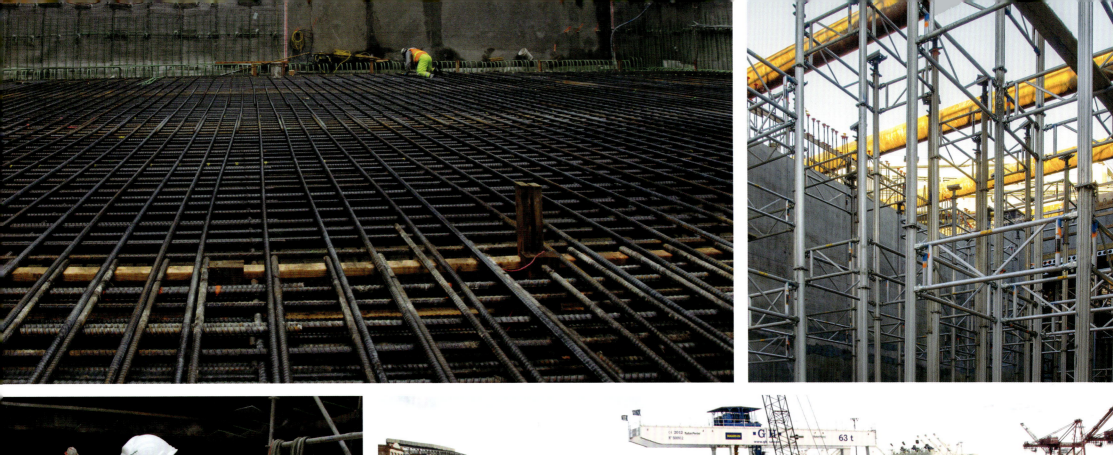

FUNCTIONS OF THE NORTH AND SOUTH OPERATIONS BUILDINGS

The North and South Operations buildings, along with WSDOT's Traffic Management Center (TMC), are key to the successful maintenance and operation of this state-of-the-art tunnel. The two buildings control the operation of the tunnel, including traffic communications, ventilation, air monitoring, and fire suppression.

The tunnel is monitored daily and controlled by tunnel operators in WSDOT's TMC in Shoreline. Operators work 24/7/365 to monitor and adjust all tunnel systems and initiate responses to incidents, accidents, or emergencies inside the tunnel. Their tools include a security and traffic camera network able to alert operators when something is out of the ordinary.

Operators can adjust traffic messaging, modify the ventilation system, activate a deluge sprinkler system inside a specific zone of the tunnel, and alert emergency responders in the event of a tunnel fire or traffic accident. WSDOT has Incident Management Response trucks stationed near the tunnel to provide fast assistance for stranded vehicles, accidents, or other incidents.

A team of maintenance engineers works out of the North Operations Building, where they too can control systems inside the tunnel when needed. Both operations buildings have emergency power capabilities to make sure the tunnel continues to function and operate in the event of a widespread power outage.

(Opposite) Early stages of the South Operations Building foundation, ground level rebar installation, cement curing, and structural steel.
(Above) Construction continues on steel structures, the installation of interior centrifugal fans, and exterior glass.

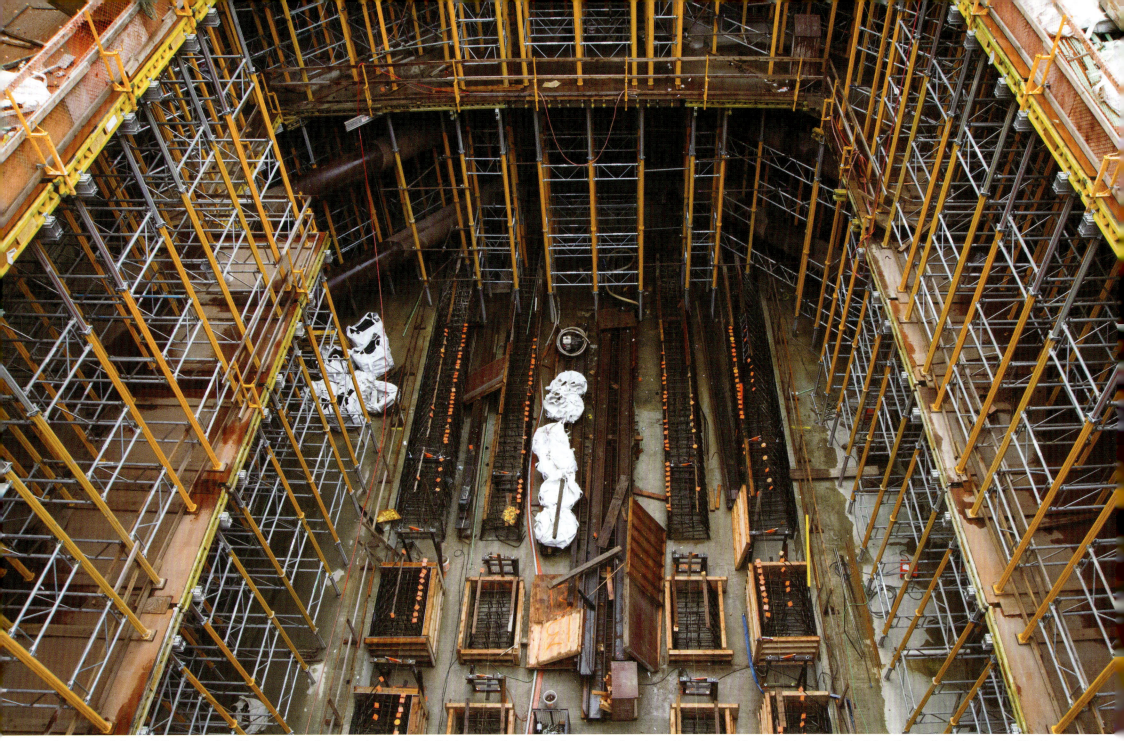

"The Forest of Shoring" illustrates the different layers of construction used to build the extraction pit. The lower elevation shows the rebar and formwork involved in building the cradle that supported Bertha once she broke in at her final destination. The geometry for the cradle had to be at the precise elevation for a smooth transition once Bertha pushed her way in. The Peri shoring that surrounded the cradle was used to build the three-foot-thick exterior walls. Once the first level of walls was formed and poured, the shoring was built. This technique constructed a work platform for the ironworkers and carpenters so they could build the next section of vertical wall. There were a total of three levels of shoring towers to reach the top of the extraction pit.

Mike Mingura, North Portal Superintendent, Tutor-Perini

NORTH PORTAL TUNNEL BORING MACHINE EXTRACTION SHAFT

Whereas the South Operations Building was built in one piece, adjacent to the tunnel launch zone, the North Operations Building was built in two sections. The main building was constructed in tandem with the deep extraction shaft at the North Portal site, in preparation for Bertha's exit at her final destination. This complex receiving shaft was 100 feet deep and took approximately two years to complete. After the exit and removal of the tunnel boring machine in the shaft, construction of the building was completed.

Nathan Burch, Superintendent, Tutor-Perini

(Top row) The North Operations Building in progress adjacent to the extraction shaft. The waterproofing of the tiebacks within the secant pile. The north corner struts on the NW corner of the extraction shaft. (Lower row) The next section of shoring for the northbound deck with the southbound deck in the foreground. Scaffolding used as a work deck so that STP could drill horizontally at the top of the tunnel eye. View of completed shaft ready for Bertha to arrive, with exterior walls, the TBM cradle, and the headwall wales and struts. The square holes within the exterior walls are the tieback block outs.

The North Operations Building is located at 6th and Thomas Street, at the site of Bertha's final destination. Both the North and South Operations Buildings provide a glowing light-show at night as the exhaust towers cycle through a rainbow of colors.

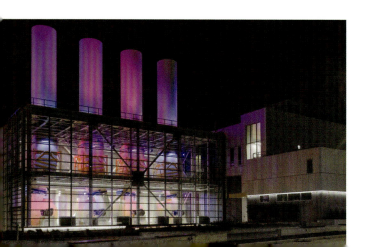

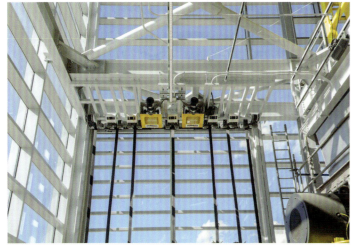

(Top) Views from the rooftop of the North Operations Building facing the landmark Space Needle. (Lower) Details of interior mechanical systems used for ventilation, monitoring controls, and safety operations.

BERTHA ARRIVAL AND EXIT

April 3, 2017 11:30 PM

Tunnel Superintendent, Tom McMahon, communicating with the pilot house inside the TBM, as Bertha approaches her destination on the morning of April 4, 2017

"The SR 99 Tunnel Project was a complex and challenging project, similar to other heavy civil underground projects constructed in an urban environment, with two notable exceptions. First, it involved using the world's largest-diameter tunnel boring machine, Bertha. And second, it attracted significant external interest and attention from politicians, the community, the media, and the tunneling industry.

When Bertha stopped in December 2013, external interest and attention increased substantially. During the subsequent two-year period until Bertha resumed tunneling in December 2015, there was concern as to whether the project would be completed. For those of us on the STP team, we never had any doubt that Bertha would resume tunneling and that the project would be successfully accomplished.

Bertha's breakthrough on April 4, 2017 commemorated completion of tunneling, but also celebrated the perseverance and hard work of the STP team that enabled the project to achieve this milestone.

In focusing on the tunneling aspect of the SR 99 Tunnel Project, it is easy to lose sight of the other major noteworthy and extraordinary construction work that occurred on the project, particularly the construction of the double-deck concrete highway structure in the tunnel at the same time that Bertha was excavating and lining the tunnel.

The people on the STP team utilized the world's largest-diameter tunnel boring machine and implemented innovative construction means and methods to successfully complete the SR 99 tunnel, Seattle's world-class infrastructure project.

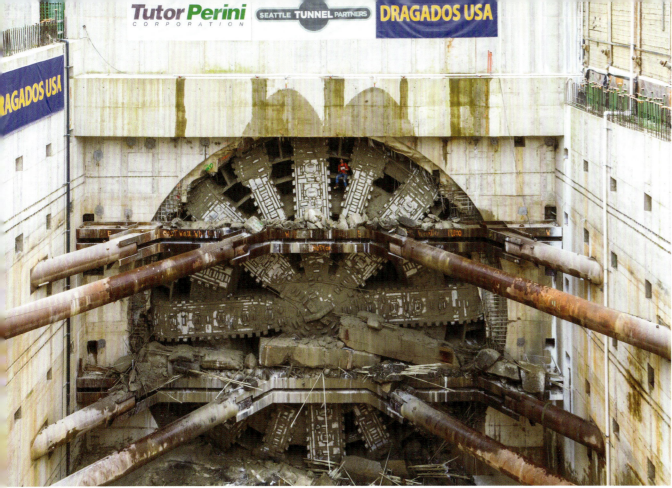

April 4, 2017 11:30 AM

As a Tutor Perini employee, I was honored and privileged to serve as the Project Manager for STP during my seven years on the project, and I was fortunate to have an STP team so committed and dedicated to doing whatever needed to be done to successfully complete the project. My lasting memories of the project will not be what we accomplished, but how we completed what we set out to do, and of all of the people on the STP team who truly made it possible, to whom I will forever be grateful for what we were able to accomplish together."

Chris Dixon
Project Manager
Seattle Tunnel Partners

Governor Jay Inslee (upper left, convenes with WSDOT and Seattle Tunnel Partners at the North Portal Exit site.

The morning of April 7, 2017 was sunny and cool. Management, crews, dignitaries, guests, and press gathered around the perimeters above the deep North Portal shaft, for the long-awaited day of Bertha's grand exit. The grinding of the TBM could be heard behind the wall of pilings. Right on target, at 9:30 AM, a sharp blast rang out; water gushed from the ground level into the shaft. Smoke and dust billowed up and out to the surrounding area. Bertha broke through and was visible as the dust cleared, turning magnificently as the pilings broke and crashed forward into the shoring system stabilizing the portal wall. As the machine came slowly to a halt, the elated shouts and whistles of the crew from within the machine marked the end of Bertha's arduous and triumphant journey.

A BEAUTIFUL SIGHT

After successfully breaking through the barrier wall, Bertha slowly pushed forward and onto the awaiting cradle support rails. Following inspection and a thorough cleaning, she was ready to greet the public.

Proud crew members, project managers, and members of the machine's manufacturer, Hitachi Zosen, raised their hats in front of the historic cutter head on April 14, 2017. A few days later, after moving to the front of the shaft and her final position, the public was invited to stop by on Visitors' Day and see Bertha after her four-year journey underground.

Dragados USA team members: Santiago Martínez, Sergio Moya, Francisco González, Jose Luis Méndez-Sánchez, Juan Luis Magro, and Jorge Vázquez at the foot of the tunnel boring machine after a successful exit at the North Portal receiving shaft.

Lead members of the Dragados USA management and engineering team gathered at the south tunnel launch site, following the triumphant breakthrough of 'Bertha' on April 4, 2017

(Left to right) Tom McMahon (General Superintendent), Cristyn Johnson (Regional HR), Tamaka Thorton (Regional Diversity Manager), Juan Luis Magro (Construction Manager), Johana Ryan (Senior Accountant), Gregory Hauser (Deputy Project Manager), Phillip Carnavale (Dragados West ESH Director), Jose Luis Méndez-Sánchez (VP West Coast Division), Juan Garnero (TBM Superintendent), Francisco González (Project Manager), Benigno Corbacho (QC Engineer), Ignacio Segura (CEO), Xavier Manjarín (QC Engineer), Julián Garvin Montealegre (Equipment Manager), Roger Escoda (Tunnel Manager), Rubén Laureano (Production/Cost Control Engineer), Santiago Martínez (Electrical Superintendent), Jorge Vázquez (Tunnel Superintendent), Sergio Moya (QC Engineer), Alejandro Arroyo (Equipment Engineer), Will Yoho (Superintendent), Al Hockaday (Safety Manager).

The tunnel boring machine on December 4, 2015 in the Access Shaft, repaired and ready to continue her underground drive. (Opposite) Bertha on display, April 13, 2017, after her successful arrival at the North Portal exit destination.

BERTHA DISASSEMBLY

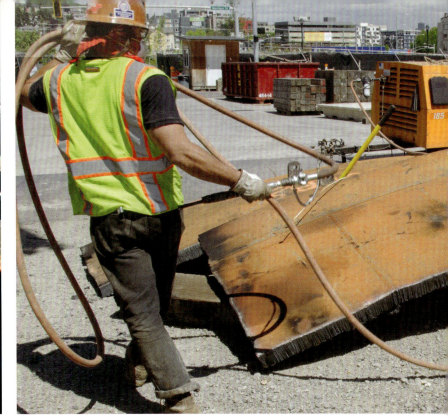

FAREWELL BERTHA

After four long and hot summer months, working 24/7, the crews removed the last portions of the historic tunnel boring machine, Bertha, in August 2017.

SPOTLIGHT
ON THE JOB

MECHANICAL WELDER, MARCEL OEDRAOGO

"I've been here since 2013, since before the TBM came from Japan. I was part of the first group unloading the TBM from the ship. We drove it to the shaft, put it down, and put it together. I work for Local 302.

I've had a chance to work with people who've been in the industry for years, 30 or 40 years. I was brand new so they had to teach me everything, step-by-step. Now I'm making my way up. I will pass that knowledge on to those who come after me. It's how we make things happen, by building a community, by helping each other, by pulling those who cannot reach. By standing up for your friends, your family, your co-workers.

We told everybody we would see the end of the tunnel. And today, this is the end of the tunnel. The biggest tunnel in the world. And we never gave up. Bertha broke down, we took it out from the ground, we fixed it, put it back, and slowly but surely we made it to the end. That's what happens when people get together as a team to build the country. And it's a blessing. It's not a chance, it's a *blessing*.

By the end of the month, no more Bertha, but the tunnel will be there. And hopefully in a year or two I will be taking my family driving through the tunnel and can say, "I helped build this." It was a long journey. But we always make it to the end. We never give up, we never give up."

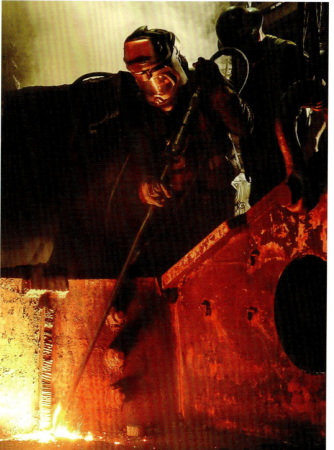

"At the end of the day, you have to go home safe. You have to go home to your family. It's a very dangerous job so you have to pay attention. And we all do, that's why we're all still here, from the beginning to the end."

Marcel and son, Kenny

The exit shaft on August 21, 2017, day of a total solar eclipse.

Following Bertha's triumphant arrival at her destination, there was much discussion about the possibility of salvaging the famous cutter head for public display. The tunnel boring machine, Bertha, was too large to remove in one piece from the North Portal Exit shaft. Even if she were cut into sections and re-assembled, the task would have been extremely difficult and costly, if at all possible. As there were no firm plans backed by funding, eventually the decision was made to dismantle her piece-by-piece, a process which took the next four months over the summer of 2017.

Crews worked around the clock, cutting the machine by oxyacetylene torch, a meticulous procedure. Two giant cranes, perched on opposite ends of the shaft, lifted each section of steel and all components of the machine and trailing gear up and out, onto the open lot where they were inspected and cleaned before being hauled away by truck. Some key pieces were salvaged for historical preservation, including the full pilot control deck suite, which was presented to Seattle's Museum of History and Industry (MOHAI) for their collection.

1,426 RINGS

Interior tunnel view to the exit shaft at the North Portal

TUNNEL SAFETY

As part of meeting the stringent safety requirements of the Washington State Department of Transportation (WSDOT), the State Route 99 tunnel is designed to be one of the safest ever constructed with state-of-the-art fire detection, suppression, ventilation systems, and a pressurized evacuation area with its own ventilation system. Together, the system works to control fires, evacuate smoke, and move people to safety.

Real-time traffic technology instructs drivers via more than 100 programmable, overhead, digital message signs to minimize delays caused by collisions, stalled vehicles, or other incidents.

Walkways inside the tunnel, separate from the roadway, provide safe evacuation routes for motorists who need to leave their vehicles. Sliding doors in alcoves, lit by bright green lights, are located every 650' on one side of the roadway. Once people enter the refuge area, they can walk out each end of the tunnel to the street level.

These areas, separated from the roadway by concrete walls, have independent ventilation and cameras, as well as emergency push-to-talk phones, that connect to emergency dispatchers. Instructions come through loudspeakers letting occupants know what to do. Cell phones and radios will work inside the tunnel. Inside the tunnel's emergency exit corridor, maintenance fans provide fresh air pressurization, preventing smoke from entering the corridor when emergency doors are opened.

Fire can be detected visually by more than 300 incident and security cameras and by a sophisticated linear heat-detection system installed in both roadway ceilings. Cameras are monitored by control center operators who have direct lines of communication to the Seattle fire and police departments and other emergency responders. The linear heat detectors will initiate alarms, which activate a zoned deluge sprinkler system that will begin working in less than 90 seconds when operators turn them on at the local control center or at the regional traffic control center in Shoreline, Washington.

A fire-resistant calcium silicate liner coats the tunnel's walls and ceilings, to limit damage to the structure from elevated steel and concrete temperatures created by heat from a fire. The water deluge, flowing at a rate of 0.3 gallons-per-minute per square foot of road area (15 times the density of a heavy 2"-per-hour rainfall), will keep extreme heat buildup to less than 716°F, as required by Seattle fire codes.

When environmental monitoring stations inside the tunnel detect vehicle emissions or particulates in the air above normal levels, the ventilation system's jet and exhaust fans will automatically activate to increase fresh air supply while minimizing system energy consumption requirements. In the event of a vehicle fire, the tunnel's eight extraction fans (500 hp each) will be turned on. The extraction fans pull out smoke through an exhaust duct via a damper that opens near the fire location to minimize smoke spread. The dampers are spaced at 110-foot intervals along the tunnel.

Power comes from two Seattle City Light substations. Should power be lost from one substation, it will be automatically fed from the other. Each building includes a diesel generator for emergency power in the event power is lost from both substations. This redundancy provides a reliable, continuous source of electricity to the tunnel systems—even in an extreme emergency.

Brian Russell, PE, Project Manager, HNTB

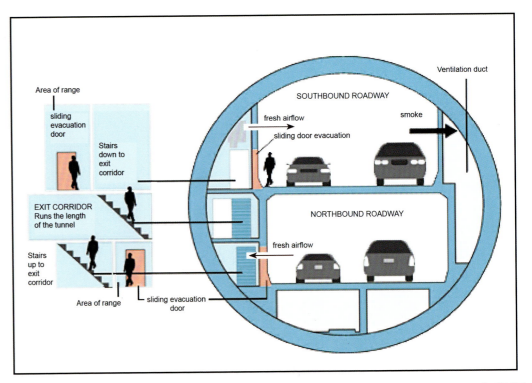

(Drawing courtesy of WSDOT)

(Above) Powerful jet fans installed at each entrance and exit of the tunnel, ensuring maximum air circulation capability. (Below) The egress interior stairwells and corridors which contain electrical, mechanical and plumbing installations and also serve as an emergency escape route.

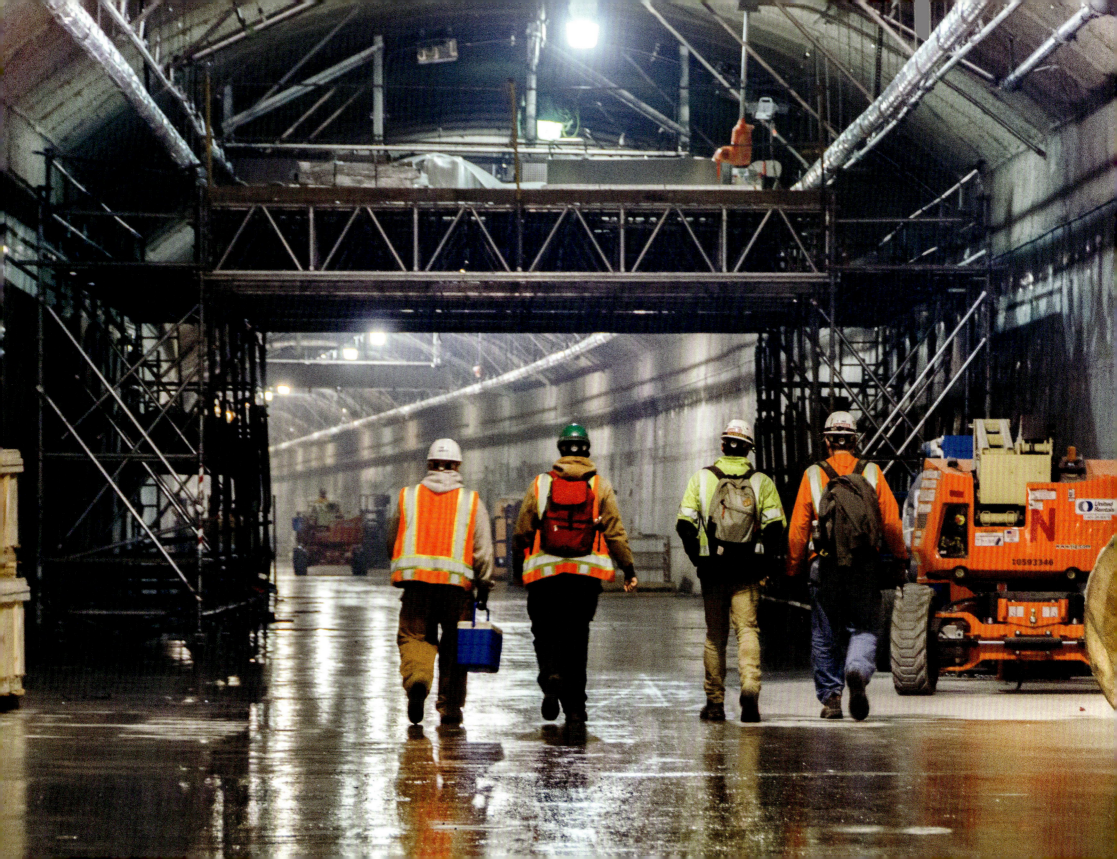

2014

2017

2018

Entrance northbound at stadium district during final construction

TUNNEL INAUGURATION

A group of City, State, and Department of Transportation officials spoke to the gathered public, eager to witness the formal ribbon-cutting ceremony and Governor Inslee's declaration that the long-awaited tunnel was now open to traffic.

The grand opening ceremony of the newly-completed tunnel was held on February 2, 2019, staged at the southbound tunnel exit with a view of the Seattle's downtown skyline beyond.

Roger Millar, Secretary of the Washington State Department of Transportation (above), addressed the crowd with opening statements, while many of the key individuals responsible for all the chapters of this historic event listened on the stage.

In attendance was former Governor Christine Gregoire (below), whose leadership was largely responsible for the decision to go forward with the Alaskan Way Viaduct Replacement Program and the tunnel.

Speakers at the podium included:

Secretary Roger Millar, WSDOT
Chairwoman Virginia Cross, Muckleshoot Indian Tribe
Chairman Leonard Forsman, Suquamish Tribe
Governor Jay Inslee, State of Washington
Dan Mathis, Federal Highway Administration
Senator Steve Hobbs, Washington State Legislature
Representative Jake Fey, Washington State Legislature
Executive Dow Constantine, King County
Commissioner Peter Steinbrueck, Port of Seattle
Councilmember Sally Bagshaw, City of Seattle

Following the ceremony, with the tunnel declared 'open', the public was free to walk the length of the tunnel on the lower-deck roadway. On their way in, they crossed paths with the crowd coming from the opposite direction, who had already walked the two-mile trek, beginning at the North Portal entrance at Harrison Street.

The closing of the 65-year-old Alaskan Way Viaduct and the opening of the tunnel was a flurry of public events, opportunities to bid farewell, and welcome the new SR 99 underground thoroughfare.

(Above) View from the south into the lower deck roadway, showing one of the emergency exits into the safety egress zone. (Below) The crowd emerging from walking the length of the tunnel on Opening Day.

Seattleites celebrated their final farewell with a drive on the Alaskan Way Viaduct—January 11, 2019—honking horns and flashing headlights.

BEHIND THE CAMERA

One morning in late January 2014, I packed my camera gear in the car and drove to the waterfront, alongside the Alaskan Way Viaduct, a road I'd taken many times before. But on this cold, drizzly day something new was afoot, as I parked at Pier 48 and walked to the trailers lining the underpass at South Dearborn Street. Here, at the main jobsite for Seattle's new underground tunnel, I was to meet with Dragados, the Spanish half of the Seattle Tunnel Partners JV, responsible for the mining of the new highway, already well underway.

Greg Hauser, Deputy Project Manager, had been there since 4 AM. He showed me a diagram of Bertha's cutter head, that of the largest tunnel boring machine in the world, explaining the concept of 'earth-pressure-balance' to my novice ears. The phone rang; he gave an update on the morning's progress. This was an important day. They were examining the tunnel boring machine, which had come to a halt in early December 2013, after mining just over 1000 feet into its two-mile journey.

My assumption that this would be a brief meeting about my duties as the on-site photographer for the project switched gears when he bolted from his chair, grabbed his coffee and said, "Let's go down into the tunnel!" The lot was a sprawling open space, covered with rows of neatly stacked giant curved concrete segments, above which hovered an ominous tower gantry. We signed in, walked to the landing of the scaffold, and started down the 100 feet of winding metal steps. Focused on keeping pace and not tripping over my steel-toe boots, it wasn't until we reached the ground that I had my first look at... the beast. The mouth of the tunnel was a breathtaking sight. Surrounded by towers of pilings pegged into the earth, holding back the earth and groundwater, we walked up and into the cavernous dark hole.

This was clearly another world. In that one morning, I was introduced to the five-story maze of the 'trailing gear', the housing of all mechanics, tasks, and procedures necessary to drive the tunnel boring machine and build the tunnel behind as it progressed. Greg pointed out the functions of all that we encountered, as we climbed the steep stairs to higher platforms, winding our way to the front, via the buzzing pilot house, the screw conveyor, the medical quarters, the compression chambers, arriving at the open floor behind the cutter head where the segment erector hung, waiting to continue building the rings of the tunnel wall.

By the time we walked our way back through the tunnel into the open air, my head was spinning. I had a million questions. Little did I know at the time that they would all be answered over what turned into six years documenting the historic project and creating this book.

While conversations were under way regarding Bertha's future, I navigated the main launch site, the tunnel interior, construction of the North Portal, and the manufacturing of the concrete segments in Frederickson. Tunnel Inspector Carl Neagoy and Environmental Specialist Pat Bagge had the occasional task of guiding me—an unexpected gift, as they managed to keep me out of harm's way and I became privy to their wealth of information.

Including the tunnel, there were six active work zones, hundreds of workers covering three shifts, heavy machinery on the ground and in the air, all day and all night. Safety protocols were strict because potential danger was real. "Nothing moves fast around here," Carl said up front. I began to meet members of the crew who, in turn, opened the most important door for a photographer on a site of that magnitude—access. With their trust, I was able to photograph without hindrance. On many occasions they went out of their way to accommodate an important shot.

This job was grand, even in the smallest detail. There was no shortage of opportunity to make the innate come alive in the lens. My career has roots in photojournalism, advertising, architecture, and design—all of which related in some way to this project. From weekly site documentation to multi-camera coverage of key milestones, photographing the tunnel made use of similar skills and added new challenges through its complexity and scale. Particularly memorable was flying in the 'man cage' high above the Viaduct or down into the 120-foot shaft, to show the big picture. It was exhilarating, and felt like a privilege. I took every opportunity to stand at the edge of the crow's nest, hanging over the abyss of the Access Shaft. I'd find myself alone, deep within the tunnel confines, when it was so quiet the click of the camera echoed.

Video added an important dimension to my routine, as I realized the scope of the project. From the racing purr of the conveyor belt, to Bertha's magnificent lifts and breakthroughs, and filming the full drive of the empty road decks—live action and sound would ultimately provide a complete archive.

I met a parade of skilled men and women whose energy was unstoppable and work ethic admirable; with whom I made enduring friendships. This book came to life as they shared their own experiences on the job.

An unusual assignment, this job was one of the most surprising, demanding, fulfilling, and thought-provoking of my career. My hope is that readers can sense the magnitude of dedicated labor and engineering that built Seattle's new tunnel.

Flag that hung at the front of the TBM interior throughout the drive beneath Seattle, signed by crew members at the end of Bertha's journey.

PROJECT CREDITS
Owner: Washington State Department of Transportation, Olympia, WA
Partners: Federal Highway Administration, King County, City of Seattle, Port of Seattle
Design/build contractor: Seattle Tunnel Partners, a joint venture of Dragados USA Inc., New York City, NY and Tutor Perini Corporation, Sylmar, CA
TBM manufacturer: Hitachi Zosen Sakai Works, Osaka, Japan
Engineering and construction management support: Mott MacDonald Group, WSP, Shannon & Wilson, McMillen Jacobs Associates, Hill International, Inc.
Lead designer and engineer of record, Tunnel and Operation and Maintenance Buildings: HNTB Corporation, Bellevue, WA
HNTB design subconsultants: Intecsa-Inarsa, S.A., Madrid, Spain; Hart Crowser, Inc., Seattle, WA; Tres West Engineers, Inc., Tacoma, WA; Integrated Design Engineers LLC, Seattle, WA; Earth Mechanics, Inc., Fountain Valley, CA; and CivilTech Engineering, Inc., Bellevue, WA

HNTB Planning and Design article:
Brian Russell, P.E., SR 99 Design Project Manager, co-authored with:
Gerald Dorn, P.E., S.E., Structural Engineer
Yang Jiang, Ph.D., P.E., S.E., Structural Tunnel Liner Engineer
Thomas Cossette, P.E., Tunnel Roadway Structural Engineer
Sean Cassady, P.E., Tunnel Ventilation and Fire Protection Engineer
David Parker, P.E., Mechanical Engineer
Andrew Herten, P.E., Construction Engineer

 In recognition of the individuals and organizations that supported my work during the documentation of the SR 99 tunnel and contributed to the creation of this book—my sincere appreciation to the hard-working crews, the labor unions, and project management.

Additionally, a special thanks to the following for their expertise and support:

Robert Armstead, Karen Armstead, Pat Bagge, Jan Babendererde, Petyr Beck, Jorge Casado, Gregory Bell, CalPortland, Reiner Decher, Chris Dixon, Dragados, Engineering News Magazine, Bobby Forch, Foss Maritime, Glazer's Camera, Roger Hagan, Gregory Hauser, History LInk, Hitachi-Zosen, Jeff Huber, Martha Kenley, Lorne McConachie, Museum of History and Industry (MOHAI), Mike Mingura, Nathan Burch, Guy Kramer, James Lindsay, Tom McMahon, Mammoet, Lisa Miller, Richard Mitchell, Rock Andrews, Carl Neagoy, Office of Minority and Women's Business Enterprises, Shinji Ogaki, Jerry Roberge, Jeremy Roller, Brian Russell, David Sowers, Peter Steinbrueck, The Seattle Tunnel Partners and administrative staff, The Seattle Times, The Washington State Department of Transportation, and Tunnel Business Magazine.

Catherine Bassetti

To my family for their unfailing encouragement and free rein to explore.

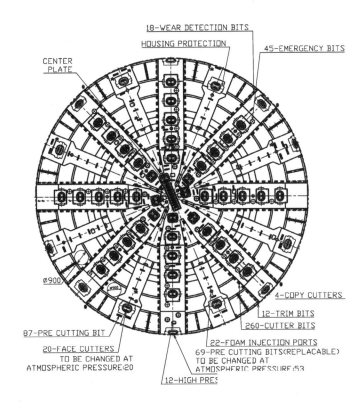
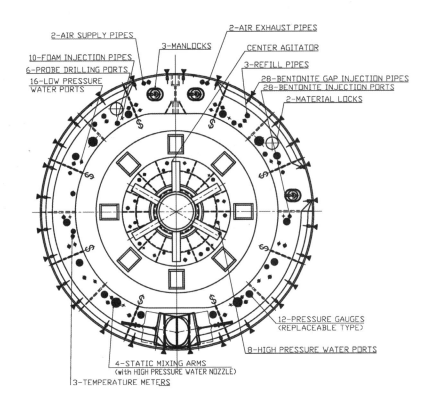
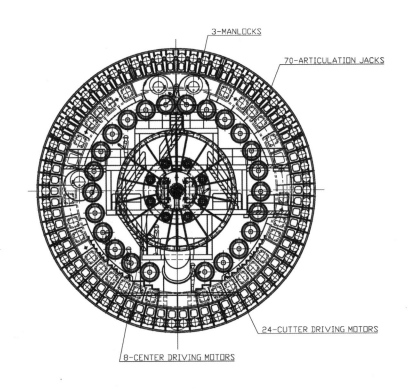